Skills Scope & Sequence

Week	1	2	3	4	5	6	7	8	9	10	11	12	13	14	15	16	17	18	19	20	21	22	23	24	25	26	27	28	29	30	31	32	33	34	35	36
Numbers																																				
base-ten system	●																																			
word/standard forms		●													●										●		●							●	●	
place value			●			●		●			●			●	●	●				●											●		●	●		
rounding		●				●		●							●		●			●				●					●			●	●		●	
estimation													●					●					●	●			●			●	●			●		
properties/number relationships	●																●	●											●		●					
factors and GCF			●			●					●				●		●	●			●		●		●	●		●	●				●		●	
multiples and LCM				●																	●				●	●			●	●		●				●
inequalities												●	●						●	●	●	●							●	●	●			●		
decimals	●	●	●	●	●	●	●	●	●	●	●	●	●	●	●	●	●	●	●	●	●	●	●	●	●	●	●	●	●	●	●	●	●	●	●	●
fractions		●	●	●					●	●	●	●		●	●	●	●	●	●	●	●	●	●	●	●	●	●	●	●	●	●	●	●	●	●	●
percents				●						●					●						●	●		●	●	●		●	●	●	●			●		●
integers				●						●		●									●	●				●			●		●			●		
exponents		●										●	●													●						●				
prime numbers																			●				●	●		●					●					
Patterns and Algebra																																				
figural patterns	●					●						●	●									●														
numerical patterns		●	●									●	●			●				●						●		●		●				●		
expressions		●	●	●				●				●																								
function tables				●			●	●																												
equations		●					●				●	●		●			●			●						●										●
Geometry/Spatial																																				
2-dimensional shapes	●	●				●				●	●	●				●	●		●										●				●	●		
3-dimensional shapes				●													●											●					●	●	●	
congruency			●					●								●	●				●		●												●	
symmetry		●				●			●						●	●					●				●		●				●					●
spatial					●	●		●	●		●			●												●				●	●	●	●	●		
angle									●		●			●		●	●						●					●	●	●	●		●	●		

Scope and sequence chart — Weeks 1–36

Week	1	2	3	4	5	6	7	8	9	10	11	12	13	14	15	16	17	18	19	20	21	22	23	24	25	26	27	28	29	30	31	32	33	34	35	36
Measurement																																				
length															●		●		●		●			●				●		●	●					●
weight		●			●				●	●									●			●				●							●			
capacity				●	●		●			●							●		●						●		●				●					●
time	●				●	●	●	●	●	●					●	●	●	●		●	●	●	●		●					●		●	●	●		
temperature	●			●					●							●									●								●		●	
money	●	●	●	●		●	●	●	●		●	●			●	●	●		●	●	●		●	●			●		●	●	●	●		●	●	
perimeter/circumference							●			●		●	●	●				●		●				●					●			●				●
area	●		●							●		●						●	●	●		●		●		●		●	●			●		●		
volume					●						●					●					●					●		●			●			●		
Data/Probability																																				
coordinate graphing			●	●			●				●				●					●	●							●					●			●
constructing graphs				●					●																				●							
interpreting graphs						●	●						●			●		●		●	●			●				●					●			
range																							●		●	●						●			●	
mode	●				●	●							●							●			●			●				●						
median	●				●																		●													
mean	●									●	●	●	●			●							●							●						
probability	●				●								●		●		●	●	●	●						●				●	●					
permutations/combinations					●		●		●	●		●	●		●		●	●	●	●		●		●	●			●				●	●	●		

EMC 755 • © Evan-Moor Corp.

What's in
Daily Math Practice

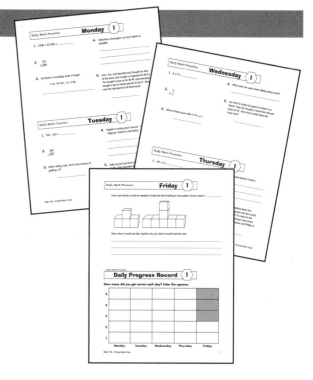

Monday through Thursday

- two computation problems

    During the first 18 weeks, the computation problems are organized as follows:
    - Monday—addition
    - Tuesday—subtraction
    - Wednesday—multiplication
    - Thursday—division

    During the second 18 weeks (weeks 19–36), the computation problems are presented in random order.

- two items that practice a variety of math skills

- one word problem

Friday

Friday's format includes one problem that is more extensive and may require multiple steps. These problems emphasize reasoning and communication in mathematics.

Also featured on Friday is a graph form where students record the number of problems they got correct each day that week.

Additional Features

Scope and Sequence

Scope and sequence charts on pages 3 and 4 detail the specific skills to be practiced and show when they will be presented. The skills included are found in math texts at this level.

Answer Key

The answer key begins on page 117.

How to Solve Word Problems Chart

Award Certificate

How to Use *Daily Math Practice*

You may want to use all of the following presentations throughout the year to keep each lesson fresh and interesting.

1. Make overhead transparencies of the lessons. Present each lesson as an oral activity with the entire class. Write answers and make corrections using an erasable marker.

   As the class becomes more familiar with *Daily Math Practice*, you may want students to mark their answers first and then check them against correct responses marked on the transparency.

2. Reproduce the pages for individuals or partners to work on independently. Check answers as a group, using an overhead transparency to model the correct answers. (Use these pages as independent practice only after much oral group experience with the lessons.)

3. Occasionally, you may want to use a day's or even a full week's lesson(s) as a test to see how individuals are progressing in their acquisition of skills.

Some Important Considerations

1. Allow students to use whatever tools they need to solve problems. Some students will choose to use manipulatives, while others will want to make drawings.

2. It is important that students be able to share their solutions. This modeling of a variety of problem-solving techniques provides a great learning benefit. Don't scrimp on the amount of time you allow for discussing how solutions were reached.

3. With the focus of the first four days being on computation and problem solving, it is recommended that calculators be used only on Fridays, when the focus is much more detailed and there is less emphasis on computation. In some instances, however, you may want to allow the use of calculators to solve the daily word problems.

Suggestions and Options

1. Sometimes you will not have taught a given skill before it appears in a lesson. These items should then be done together. Tell the class that you are going to work on a skill they have not yet been taught. Use the practice time to conduct a minilesson on that skill.

2. Customize the daily lessons to the needs of your class.

   - If there are skills that are not included in the grade-level expectancies of the particular program you teach, you may choose to skip those items.

   - If you feel your class needs more practice than is provided, add these "extras" on your own in the form of a one-item warm-up or posttest.

3. Many of the Friday problems are quite challenging and lend themselves to partner or small-group collaboration.

EMC 755 • © Evan-Moor Corp.

1. 1,248 + 53,283 = 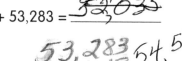 _54,531_

53,035

53,283
1,248 54,531

52,035

2.   951
      + 564
      1515

3. List these in increasing order of length.

7 cm, 18 mm, 1 m, 3 dm

_____

4. Describe a rectangle in as much detail as possible.

2 sides equal
2 sides equal

_____

_____

5. Sam, Tim, and Hernaldo each bought an item at the store. Sam bought a magazine for $2.47, Tim bought a race car for $8.99, and Hernaldo bought a set of colored pencils for $6.47. What was the total spent by all three boys?

2.47
8.99
6.47
$17.93

$17.93

1. 742 – 631 = ___111___

742
631
111

2.   589
      – 257
      332

3. When rolling a die, what is the chance of getting a 3?

_____

4. Explain in writing what "borrow," "trade," or "regroup" means in subtraction.

_____

_____

_____

5. Sally just got back from a vacation with her family. They had been driving for 3 days, traveling $8\frac{1}{2}$ hours each day. How many hours were they in the car altogether?

8.5
3
25.5

1. 8 x 9 = _____ 12

2. 4
   x 7
   ___
   28

3. What is three hours after 11:45 A.M.?

   _____ 2:45 _____

4. What units are used when talking about area?

   _____ sq ft or inch _____

5. Ian had 13 toads and gave 8 of them to a friend. Then Ian bought 6 more from the pet store for $7. How many toads does Ian have now?

   _____
   13
   - 8
   ___
   5
   + 6
   ___
   11

1. 48 ÷ 8 = _____ 6

2. 6)30
   5

3. What is 25 degrees lower than 57°F?

   _____ 32° _____

4. Explain in writing what division means.

   _____

   _____

   _____

5. Susan and Phillip are walking down the sidewalk, attempting to jump over the cracks. If there are 8 houses with 14 cracks in the sidewalk in front of each house, how many cracks are there in all for Susan and Phillip to jump over?

   _____ 112 _____

EMC 755 • © Evan-Moor Corp.

Friday <1>

10

How many blocks would be needed to build the third building in the pattern shown below? _____

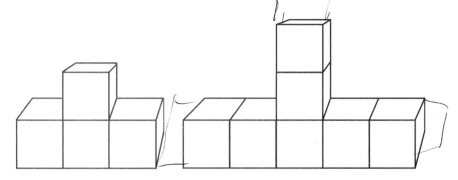

Show what it would look like. Explain why you think it would look this way.

_____

_____

_____

Daily Math Practice

Daily Progress Record <1>

How many did you get correct each day? Color the squares.

	Monday	Tuesday	Wednesday	Thursday	Friday
5					▓▓
4					▓▓
3					▓▓
2					
1					

1. 2,368 + 59 = _2427_

+ 59
2427

2368

2. 15,368
+ 2,763
18,131

3. What is half of 18?

9

4. Tell two different ways to make 37¢.

25 + 10 + 2

10 + 10 + 10 + 5 + 2

5. If Min were to buy 6 dolls for her friends and each one cost $6.27, how much money would she need?

6.27
6
37.62

1. 968 − 53 = _915_

− 53
915

2. 1,682
− 795
887

3. Write this number in standard notation.

six thousand twenty-five

6,025

4. Round 3,658 to the nearest hundred.

3600 3700

5. Scott runs on a daily basis. He jogs 6 miles every day except Saturday, when he jogs 8 miles. How many miles will he jog in three weeks?

132

36
8
44
3
132

EMC 755 • © Evan-Moor Corp.

1. 14 × 12 = _168_ $\begin{array}{r} 14 \\ 12 \\ \hline 28 \\ 14 \end{array}$

2. 3^2 = _9_

3. Complete this function table.

Input	Output
1	2
2	4
3	6
4	8
5	10
10	20
14	28

4. Jasmine bowled five games and had scores of 182, 195, 98, 175, and 182. Which measure of central tendency (mean, median, mode) is best to use to convince someone that Jasmine is a good bowler?

_____

5. Samantha wants to buy a new CD that costs $14.99. She currently has $6.25. How much more money does she need to buy the CD?

_$8.74_

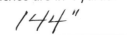

$\begin{array}{r} 14.99 \\ 6.25 \\ \hline 8.74 \end{array}$

---

1. 56 ÷ 7 = _8_

2. $\overset{104}{4\overline{)416}}$

3. Draw a square below and then draw as many lines of symmetry as possible.

4. How many inches are in 4 yards?

_144"_

$\begin{array}{r} 36 \\ 4 \\ \hline 144 \end{array}$

5. Jim walks pets. He charges $2 per small dog and $3 per large dog. On Saturday he walked 3 small dogs and 4 large dogs. How much money did he earn?

_$18_

$\begin{array}{r} 6 \\ 12 \end{array}$

Sofia is learning to knit. She makes three stitches, then checks to see if they are correct. She realizes she has to undo the last two. She then makes three more stitches and again has to undo the last two. If this pattern continues, how many stitches will Sofia have to make before she has six good stitches?

Do your work here.

Write your answer here.

Daily Progress Record ⟨2⟩

How many did you get correct each day? Color the squares.

	Monday	Tuesday	Wednesday	Thursday	Friday
5					
4					
3					
2					
1					

EMC 755 • © Evan-Moor Corp.

1. 5.73 + 3.26 = _8.99_

3.26
8.99

4. What place value does the 3 have in 235,468?

10 Thousands

2.   3.25
  + 11.73
  ~~14.98~~ *14.98*

5. Paul is putting away ten dishes. He can only fit three dishes in each stack in the cupboard. What is the minimum number of stacks he will have?

_4_

3. What are the next three terms in this pattern?

3, 6, 9, 12, _15_, _18_, _21_

---

1. 8.49 − 5.25 = _3.24_

8.49
5.25
3.24

4. Fill in the correct symbol.

< = >

25 ◯ 38

2.   6.82
  − 1.75
  507   *5.07*

5. Raul plans to go to an amusement park on Saturday. The roller coaster costs 75¢ per ride, the Ferris wheel costs 50¢ per ride, and the merry-go-round costs 15¢ per ride. If Raul has $1.35, can he ride all three rides? Explain why or why not.

3. What are all the factors of 12?

_____

75
50
15
140

_____

_____

_____

1. 5 × 6 = _30_

2.
  8
× 3
  24

3. What is the value of *n* in this equation?

$$n + 6 = 14$$

_N = 8_

4. What is the ordered pair of point **X** on this graph?

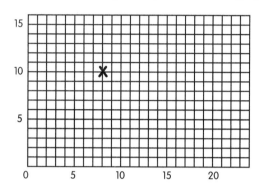

_____

5. If Cindy's mom is 35 and Cindy is 23 years younger than her mom, how old is Cindy?

  35
  23

_12_

1. 24 ÷ 4 = _6_

2. 3)27 _9_

3. Define in your own words what it means when two figures are congruent.

_____

_____

_____

4. If a rectangle is 3 inches by 5 inches, what is its area?

_15 sq"_

5. Four friends are sharing a pack of gum that contains 20 sticks of gum. How many sticks of gum will each person receive?

_5_

Friday ⟨3⟩

Betty gets paid 25¢ per paper to deliver newspapers in her neighborhood. When Betty is sick, she pays her brother Bobby 10¢ per paper to deliver them for her. If Bobby makes $7.80 filling in for Betty, how much money does Betty get to keep for that day?

Do your work here.

15¢

15 ⟌ 7.80   .52
      75
      30

Write your answer here.

Daily Progress Record ⟨3⟩

How many did you get correct each day? Color the squares.

	Monday	Tuesday	Wednesday	Thursday	Friday
5					
4					
3					
2					
1					

Monday 4

1. 12,594 + 145,682 = _____

$$12,594$$
$$145,682$$
$$158,276$$

2.   1,569
       + 862

   2,431

3. If a rectangle is 4 cm x 5 cm, what is its perimeter?

_____ 18 cm

4. If the outside temperature was 72° yesterday and today it is 16 degrees cooler, what is today's temperature?

_____ 56°

5. John has three more pet birds than he has cats. If he has 11 pets in all, how many cats does he have?

_____

Tuesday 4

1. 5,568 – 875 = _____

2.   5.26
       – 1.88

3. Given this table, construct a graph to represent the information. Use a sheet of graph paper.

Favorite Type of Drink	Number of Girls	Number of Boys
Cola	23	28
Grape	15	18
Cherry	28	22
Root Beer	12	18

4. If $x = 3$, what value does this expression have?

$$5 + x - 2$$

6

_____

5. Sue plays on a soccer team. On a particular Saturday, she scored 8 goals. This was one-fourth of the goals she scored during the entire season. How many goals did she score during the entire season?

_____

EMC 755 • © Evan-Moor Corp.

Wednesday 4

1. 6 x 2 = _____12_____

2.   52
     x 3
     156

3. What are the first four multiples of 3?

   _____

4. Name three real-world objects that have the shape of a sphere.

   _____

   _____

   _____

5. Jack is learning to play the piano, which has 88 keys. If there are 12 unique keys in each octave, how many complete octaves are on the piano?

   _____

Thursday 4

1. 42 ÷ 6 = _____

2. 5)‾45‾

3. Which is heavier, a kilogram or a gram?

   _____

4. If someone says that a jacket is 25% off, what does that mean?

   _____

   _____

   _____

5. April and Amy are twin sisters. They have a total of 120 CDs. If Amy has twice as many CDs as April, how many CDs do they each have?

   _____

Friday ⟨4⟩

Mentally compute the following product (without using a calculator and without figuring it out the traditional way). After you have the answer, write down the steps that you mentally went through to find this product.

What is 25 x 17? _____

_____

_____

_____

_____

_____

_____

Daily Progress Record ⟨4⟩

How many did you get correct each day? Color the squares.

	Monday	Tuesday	Wednesday	Thursday	Friday
5					
4					
3					
2					
1					

1. 5.29 + 6.73 = _____

2. 6.29
      + 9.68

3. What is the median of this data?

4, 6, 7, 9, 10, 12, 14, 15, 15

_____

4. How many quarts are in a gallon?

_____

5. Brandon is half as old as his brother Ryan. Ryan is one-eighth the age of his father. If their father is 32 years old, how old are Ryan and Brandon?

_____

1. 5.26 − 4.15 = _____

2. 5.6
      − 1.8

3. If a cube is 3 inches on each edge, what is its volume?

_____

4. What does it mean if an angle is a right angle?

_____

_____

_____

5. Beth is cooking pizzas and cuts each one into 8 pieces. If she has 14 people coming to her house for dinner and she thinks that each person will eat 3 slices of pizza, how many pizzas should she make?

_____

Wednesday ⟨5⟩

1. 1.2 × 3 = _____

2. 10
      × 3
     ─────

3. What are the chances of rolling an even number on a six-sided die?

_____

4. How many sides does an octagon have?

_____

5. David and his two brothers deliver papers every morning. Each one of them can deliver a paper every two minutes, and between the three of them they deliver 147 papers. How long does it take them to deliver the papers?

_____

Thursday ⟨5⟩

1. 72 ÷ 9 = _____

2. 5)120

3. How many different two-letter initials can be made using the letters *d*, *g*, *m*, *s*, and *t* if you can use each letter only once in each initial?

_____

4. What is the mode of this data?

4, 6, 7, 9, 10, 12, 14, 15, 15

_____

5. Naomi is half as tall as her mother. If Naomi is 2 feet, 8 inches tall, how tall is her mother?

_____

Friday ⟨5⟩

Tabitha is raising rabbits to sell during the spring. She has 16 rabbits and feeds them each one-half cup of alfalfa pellets every morning. The bag of pellets she bought completely filled a five-gallon plastic barrel. How many days will it last? (Remember that four cups equals one quart, and four quarts equals one gallon.)

Show your work here.

Write your answer here.

Daily Progress Record ⟨5⟩

How many did you get correct each day? Color the squares.

	Monday	Tuesday	Wednesday	Thursday	Friday
5					
4					
3					
2					
1					

1. 5.6 + 4.52 = _____

2.   1,825
   +   64

3. What are the next three figures in this pattern?

 △ ◯ ◯ △ ◯ ◯ △ ___ ___ ___

4. What is the mean of this data?

      4, 5, 7, 8, 11, 13

_____

5. Nick was riding on his bicycle when he saw a strange animal in the park. He noticed that the animal had five babies with it, each one looking like the parent and staring back at him. The strangest thing about these critters was that they each had 3 eyes on their heads. How many eyes in all did Nick see staring at him?

_____

---

1. 7,125 – 493 = _____

2.   2.5
   – 0.29

3. When you write $1.35, what does the decimal point mean?

_____

_____

_____

4. What place value does the 5 have in 13,542?

_____

5. Colin and his sister Cathy are cleaning their house on Saturday morning. Their house has nine rooms in it. They figure it takes one person about 8 minutes to clean one room. How long will it take them to clean the whole house if they work together the whole time?

_____

1. $4 \times 6 =$ _____

2.
$$\begin{array}{r} 200 \\ \times\ \ 4 \\ \hline \end{array}$$

3. What number sentences can be created using 3, 5, and 8?

_____

_____

_____

4. Which of these lettered figures goes in the white space?

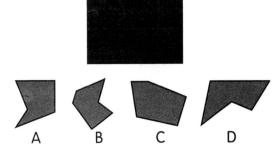

A   B   C   D

5. Vickie is going to the store to buy a few items for her mom. She will buy a loaf of bread for $1.73, a bag of cookies for $2.19, and a dozen eggs for $1.27. What will be the total of these items?

_____

---

1. $56 \div 8 =$ _____

2. $2\overline{)1.20}$

3. Round 35,894 to the nearest thousand.

_____

4. How many lines of symmetry does an equilateral triangle have?

_____

5. Steve wants to buy a new stereo. The city that he lives in charges a 5% sales tax, so for every $100 he spends, he has to pay a tax of $5. If the stereo he wants costs $250, how much tax will he have to pay?

_____

Friday 6

Given this graph, decide what it could be representing. Label the axes and tell everything you can infer from the graph.

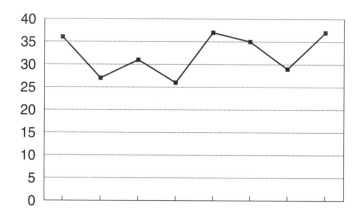

_____

_____

_____

_____

Daily Math Practice

Daily Progress Record 6

How many did you get correct each day? Color the squares.

	Monday	Tuesday	Wednesday	Thursday	Friday
5					
4					
3					
2					
1					

Monday ⟨7⟩

1. $5.8 + 6.59 =$ _____

2. $\begin{array}{r} 6.29 \\ + 2.5 \\ \hline \end{array}$

3. What is 25 hours past 9:00 A.M.?

_____

4. Write the rule for the function represented by this table.

Input	Output
3	12
4	16
5	20
6	24
7	28

_____

5. Pamela and Linda share a locker at their school. If each girl has seven classes and every class requires two books, how many books are in the locker?

_____

Tuesday ⟨7⟩

1. $2.53 - 0.1 =$ _____

2. $\begin{array}{r} 2.39 \\ - 0.806 \\ \hline \end{array}$

3. Write this number in standard notation.

thirteen thousand five

_____

4. What is the value of m in this equation?

$$5 \times m = 60$$

_____

5. Brigit has five different pairs of pants or slacks hanging in her closet. In addition to these, she has six different shirts hanging in her closet. If she wants to wear a different combination of clothing every day, how many days can she go before having to wear an identical outfit a second time?

_____

Wednesday 7

1. 7 × 8 = _____

2.   1.6
     x 3
     ‾‾‾‾

3. Plot the point (18, 7) on this coordinate plane.

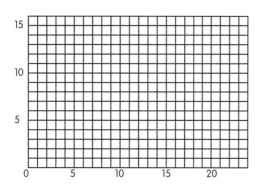

4. What is the range of this data?

35, 39, 25, 57, 62, 46, 53, 41

_____

5. Tyler has 15 more baseball cards than John. John has 6 fewer baseball cards than Juan. If Juan has 24 baseball cards, how many does Tyler have?

_____

Thursday 7

1. 25 ÷ 5 = _____

2. 5)3.5‾

3. How many grams are in a kilogram?

_____

4. What is the perimeter of this figure?

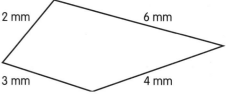

2 mm   6 mm

3 mm   4 mm

_____

5. Peter is having a terrible day. On the way to school, he lost his lunch money. He figures if he can get thirteen of his friends to each give him a dime, he can buy a school lunch. How much does a school lunch cost?

_____

Friday ⟨7⟩

Stephen has just built a doghouse. He decides that it needs some carpet to help keep his dog warm during the cold winter months ahead. He measures the rectangular-shaped floor of the doghouse and gets a perimeter of 122 inches. If the width is 25 inches, what is the area of the carpet that he needs to cover the floor of the doghouse?

Show your work here.

Write your answer here.

Daily Math Practice

Daily Progress Record ⟨7⟩

How many did you get correct each day? Color the squares.

	Monday	Tuesday	Wednesday	Thursday	Friday
5					
4					
3					
2					
1					

Monday ⟨8⟩

1. 5.49 + 12.26 = _____

2. 1.8
     + 0.253

3. Draw all possible lines of symmetry on this figure.

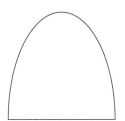

4. If $a = 3$ and $b = 2$, what value does this expression have?

$$11 + a - b$$

_____

5. Brad is going on a vacation with his family. He will be going through six states on his trip, but traveling only 900 miles. The vacation will last twenty-three days. While Brad is pleased to be missing school, his teacher has asked him to write in his journal one-half page each day of his trip. How many pages will Brad have written in his journal when he gets back home?

_____

Tuesday ⟨8⟩

1. 846,293 − 125,181 = _____

2. 8.26
     − 1.95

3. Fill in the correct symbol.

< = >

0.6 ◯ 0.60

4. List all the factors of 8.

_____

5. Heather is collecting beanbag animals. She started her collection with 6 beanbag animals just 8 weeks ago. During each of those 8 weeks, she has been given two additional beanbag animals. How many does she have at the end of the 8th week?

_____

 EMC 755 • © Evan-Moor Corp.

1. 6 x 6 = _____

2.   122
     x   6

3. Write 378 in word form.

_____

4. What place value does the 6 have in 12.6?

_____

5. Katie wants to buy six pencils from the school store. If each pencil costs 15¢, how much money does she need?

_____

1. 64 ÷ 2 = _____

2. 12)288

3. What are the next three numbers in this pattern?

1, 2, 4, 8, _____, _____, _____

4. Circle the letter of the triangle that is congruent to the first one.

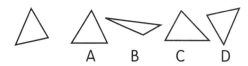

A   B   C   D

5. Fred and Ethel watched TV for several hours one afternoon. They began at 1:30 P.M. and continued watching TV for 3 hours and 45 minutes until their mom came and turned off the TV. At what time did their mom turn off the TV?

_____

Friday 8

Neal's teacher is giving away four movie tickets. The four students going to the movie are Neal, Tim, Sally, and Judy. If the two boys want to sit on either end of the four seats, in how many possible ways can they arrange themselves?

_____

Write the possible seating arrangements.

_____

_____

_____

_____

_____

_____

Daily Progress Record 8

How many did you get correct each day? Color the squares.

	Monday	Tuesday	Wednesday	Thursday	Friday
5					
4					
3					
2					
1					

1. 0.89 + 13.2 = _____

2. 12.2
   + 2.305

3. Find the circumference of a circle with a radius of 4 cm. Use 3.14 for π.

   _____

4. Order these lengths from shortest to longest.

   1 yard, 2 feet, 16 inches, 1 foot, $\frac{1}{2}$ yard

   _____

5. Timmy and Jerod are eating cupcakes. If they each can eat 2 cupcakes in 3 minutes, how long will it take the two of them to eat 18 cupcakes?

   _____

1. 2.85 − 0.4 = _____

2. 6.58
   − 0.9

3. It was 47°F when Tanya got out of bed this morning. If the temperature rose 18 degrees by lunchtime, what temperature was it then?

   _____

4. Circle the letter under each acute angle.

   A   B   C   D

5. Suzy is braiding her hair into 48 little braids. If it takes her 4 minutes to braid each one, how long will it take her to braid all 48 braids?

   _____

Wednesday ⟨9⟩

1. $9 \times 5 =$ _____

2. $\begin{array}{r} 520 \\ \times 9 \\ \hline \end{array}$

3. What are the first three multiples of 6?

_____

4. Round 35,983 to the nearest thousand.

_____

5. Missy loves to read novels. She devoured 6 books last weekend, 5 books the weekend before that, and 7 books the weekend before that. If the books averaged 120 pages, about how many pages did she read over those three weekends?

_____

Thursday ⟨9⟩

1. $54 \div 9 =$ _____

2. $3\overline{)1.26}$

3. Construct a graph for this data. Use a sheet of graph paper.

Month	Number of New Customers
January	215
February	189
March	230
April	245
May	250
June	270

4. If Sam, Joe, and Debbie each flip a coin, how many possible outcomes are there? (Hint: If Sam gets heads and the other two get tails, this is a different outcome than if Joe gets heads and the other two get tails.)

_____

5. Jon is baking a cake. The recipe calls for $1\frac{1}{2}$ cups of flour, and Jon wants to triple the recipe. How much flour does he need?

_____

Friday 9

Al, Jeff, and Linda are walking their pets in the park. The pets are a dog, a cat, and a rabbit. The names of the pets are Rocky, Fluffy, and Chunk. Read the following clues to determine the name and kind of pet each owner has.

1. Al does not own the rabbit.

2. Linda owns either Fluffy or Chunk.

3. Jeff owns the cat.

4. The cat's name is Chunk.

	dog	cat	rabbit	Rocky	Fluffy	Chunk
Al						
Linda						
Jeff						

Daily Math Practice

Daily Progress Record 9

How many did you get correct each day? Color the squares.

	Monday	Tuesday	Wednesday	Thursday	Friday
5					
4					
3					
2					
1					

Monday ⬡10⬡

1. $^-16 + 8 =$ _____

2. $\frac{1}{4}$
   $+ \frac{1}{4}$
   _____

3. What two-dimensional figure has three sides, two of which are the same length?

   _____

4. What is 20% of 300?

   _____

5. Stu had quite a collection of baseball cards. One day he decided to give half of them to his brother Seth. Then he gave one-third of what he had left to a friend. Then he gave half of what was left to another friend. Stu now has 50 baseball cards. How many did he start with?

   _____

Tuesday ⬡10⬡

1. $2 - 0.69 =$ _____

2. $\frac{5}{8}$
   $- \frac{3}{8}$
   _____

3. Order these weights from lightest to heaviest.

   1 g, 1 kg, 1 mg

   _____

4. Find the area of a circle with a radius of 7 inches. Use 3.14 for π.

   _____

5. Gary is planning to make 7 cuts in a loaf of bread. He is making each slice of bread 1 inch thick. How long is the loaf of bread?

   _____

1. $6.2 \times 0.5 =$ _____

4. How many liters are in 7 kiloliters?

_____

2. $\begin{array}{r} ^-7 \\ \times\ 7 \\ \hline \end{array}$

5. Juan's height is 15 inches less than Suzanne's. Suzanne's height is 3 inches more than Dan's. If Dan is 58 inches tall, how tall are Suzanne and Juan?

_____

3. What is the probability of drawing a red card out of a deck of 52 cards, given a standard deck of 52 cards with four suits (2 red and 2 black) with 13 cards in each suit?

_____

1. $16 \div (^-2) =$ _____

4. Draw the other three parts of this shape, given that it has these two lines of symmetry.

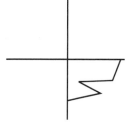

2. $10\overline{)630}$

3. What is the area of a right triangle that has legs 7 cm and 4 cm long?

_____

5. How many different outfits can George make if he has three shirts and two pairs of pants?

_____

Solve this puzzle.

Four men board a ship, each with one wife. Each couple has two kids, each kid has three cats, and each cat has five kittens.

How many mouths are there to feed, including the people and the animals? _____

How many feet are there? _____

Daily Math Practice

Daily Progress Record ⟨**10**⟩

How many did you get correct each day? Color the squares.

	Monday	Tuesday	Wednesday	Thursday	Friday
5					▓
4					▓
3					▓
2					
1					

1. $\frac{1}{3} + \frac{2}{3} =$ _____

2. $\begin{array}{r} \frac{3}{5} \\ + \frac{1}{5} \\ \hline \end{array}$

3. What is the volume of a rectangular prism that is 3 inches x 2 inches x 4 inches?

   _____

4. What are complementary angles?

   _____

   _____

5. Anne reaches in her pocket and finds 15 pennies, 9 nickels, 14 dimes, 15 quarters, and 3 one-dollar bills. How much money does she have altogether?

   _____

1. $\frac{7}{9} - \frac{5}{9} =$ _____

2. $\begin{array}{r} 5\frac{3}{7} \\ - 2\frac{1}{7} \\ \hline \end{array}$

3. What place value does the 8 have in 124.68?

   _____

4. The commutative property of addition allows one to say that 3 + 6 is the same as what?

   _____

5. Mr. Steward has a jar in which each of his 26 students has placed a stick with his or her name on it. If there are 10 girls in the class, what is the probability that a boy's name will be drawn if Mr. Steward draws one stick from the jar?

   _____

1. 0.123 x 2 = _____

2.   200
     x   21

3. What two-dimensional figure has opposite sides parallel and four right angles, but not four equal sides?

_____

4. What are the next three numbers in this pattern?

5, 9, 13, 17, ____, ____, ____

5. List all the factors of 6 and 8, then find the GCF (greatest common factor).

_____

_____

_____

---

1. 12⟌756

2. Fill in the correct symbol.

< = >

6.3 ◯ 2.47

3. Use a factor tree to write the prime factors of 120.

4. Graph the points (3, 2), (7, 6), and (9, 8) on this coordinate graph.

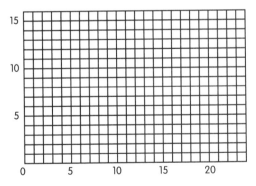

5. Are the three points in problem 4 collinear?

_____

EMC 755 • © Evan-Moor Corp.

Friday ⟨11⟩

Four children—Cindy, Tim, Sally, and Scott—whose last names are Bartlet, Brown, Hughes, and Miller are each going on a family vacation. Their destinations are Florida, South Dakota, Colorado, and California and they are traveling by bus, plane, van, or car. Read the following clues to determine the first and last name, the destination, and the means of transportation for each child.

1. The Hughes girl went by car.
2. The family going to South Dakota went by van.
3. Sally went to California.
4. The Miller boy went by bus.
5. Scott went to Colorado.
6. Neither the car, nor the Bartlets, nor Scott went to California.
7. Tim's last name is NOT Miller.

Daily Progress Record ⟨11⟩

How many did you get correct each day? Color the squares.

	Monday	Tuesday	Wednesday	Thursday	Friday
5					
4					
3					
2					
1					

1. $\frac{3}{8} + \frac{4}{8} =$ _____

2. $\begin{array}{r} {}^{-}9 \\ +\ 11 \\ \hline \end{array}$

3. How do you know if a number is divisible by 2?

_____

_____

4. Round 2,589,462 to the nearest ten thousand.

_____

5. Jenny's father works at the local grocery store. He just finished setting up a display of soup cans in the shape of a triangle. There are 4 cans of soup in the top row. For each of the following rows, he added 2 cans of soup to each end, so there are 8 cans of soup in the second row, 12 in the third row, and so forth. How many cans of soup are in the 12th row?

_____

1. $5\frac{9}{11} - 2\frac{4}{11} =$ _____

2. $\begin{array}{r} 6\frac{2}{5} \\ -\ 2\frac{1}{5} \\ \hline \end{array}$

3. What are supplementary angles?

_____

_____

4. Are all squares rectangles?

_____

Are all rectangles squares?

_____

5. Mary and Tom were buying a present for their mother for Mother's Day. Mary spent $12 and Tom spent $28. If they wanted to share the cost equally, how much money does Mary owe Tom?

_____

 EMC 755 · © Evan-Moor Corp.

Wednesday 12

1. $9^2 =$ _____

2. $\begin{array}{r} 1.2 \\ \times\ 0.26 \\ \hline \end{array}$

3. What is the perimeter of an equilateral triangle whose sides measure 7.5 centimeters?

   _____

4. Fill in the blank.

   $6.02 + 1.3 -$ _____ $= 4.39$

5. A restaurant in town offers you a free meal after 8 visits, so the 9th meal is free. How many meals will you have eaten at this restaurant once you have finished eating your 5th free meal?

   _____

Thursday 12

1. $(^-81) \div (^-9) =$ _____

2. $4\overline{)1.28}$

3. What is the mean of this data?

   14, 27, 30, 35, 38

   _____

4. What value would m have in this equation to make it true?

   $5 \times m = 15$

   _____

5. If a rectangle measures 16 inches by 1 foot, what is its area?

   _____

Friday ⟨12⟩

How many three-digit numbers can you create with 3, 6, 7, and 9, using each digit only once in every number?

_____

What is the smallest three-digit number you can create using these digits, and how do you know it is the smallest possible?

_____

Daily Progress Record ⟨12⟩

How many did you get correct each day? Color the squares.

	Monday	Tuesday	Wednesday	Thursday	Friday
5					
4					
3					
2					
1					

  EMC 755 • © Evan-Moor Corp.

Monday ⬡13

1. $5\frac{1}{4} + 2\frac{1}{4} =$ _____

2. $\quad 2\frac{1}{5}$
   $+\ 3\frac{4}{5}$

3. What is the mode of this data?

   88, 89, 96, 89, 90, 90, 88, 89, 92, 94, 90

   _____

4. Find the least common multiple (LCM) of 4 and 6.

   _____

5. Given this graph, about how many more people voted for the most popular candidate than for the least popular one?

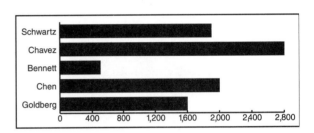

   _____

Tuesday ⬡13

1. $25,492 - 18,900 =$ _____

2. $\quad \frac{7}{8}$
   $-\ \frac{4}{8}$

3. Evaluate this expression for $a = 3$.

   $a^2 + a$

   _____

4. What are the next two figures in this pattern?

   _____   _____

5. How many 3-digit numbers can be made using the digits 4, 6, 7, and 9? (You can use each digit only once in every number.)

   _____

1. $\frac{1}{2} \times \frac{1}{4} =$ _____

2. 482
   x 42

3. Simplify this expression. (Remember the order of operations when solving this problem.)

   $4 + (5 \times 2) - 3$

   _____

4. What are the next four numbers in this pattern?

   3, 7, 6, 10, 9, 13, 12, ____, ____, ____, ____

   Explain the pattern.

   _____

   _____

5. Ethan went bowling and had these scores: 128, 97, 123, and 108. What was his average?

   _____

1. $1.8 \div 3 =$ _____

2. $3\overline{)1,254}$

3. Given this spinner, what is the probability of getting a B?

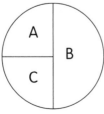

   _____

4. Using the spinner in problem 3, what is the probability of getting a vowel?

   _____

5. In a pasture are horses and chickens. If there are a total of 28 heads and 80 legs, how many chickens and how many horses are in the pasture?

   _____

EMC 755 • © Evan-Moor Corp.

Friday

A city has a circular wall surrounding it. Within the city are four buildings that are visible over the wall. The four buildings look like this:

An artist wants to draw what the city looks like from outside the wall on the northeast side. The only available pictures show south and west views of the city. They look like this:

This view is from the south:

This view is from the west:

What will the artist's sketch look like from the northeast?

Daily Math Practice

Daily Progress Record 〈13〉

How many did you get correct each day? Color the squares.

	Monday	Tuesday	Wednesday	Thursday	Friday
5					
4					
3					
2					
1					

1. 12,289 + 8,361 = _____

2. $\frac{1}{2}$
$+ \frac{1}{4}$
_____

3. Write this number in standard form.

three hundred forty-five and six tenths

_____

4. How do you know if a number is divisible by 5?

_____

_____

5. Roger is going to have a party at his house. He is inviting three times as many girls as boys. If he is inviting 16 people, how many boys and how many girls will there be?

_____

1. 5.29 − 0.008 = _____

2. $\frac{1}{2}$
$- \frac{1}{4}$
_____

3. How many blocks does it take to build this building?

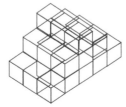

4. If the product of two numbers is 12 and the sum is 7, what are the two numbers?

_____

5. The Wildcats scored an average of 56 points per game during their four-game season. If the scores for their first three games were 48, 57, and 52, what was the score of their last game?

_____

_____

Wednesday ⟨14⟩

1. 29 x 21 = _____

2. 2.5
x 0.6

3. Find the outer perimeter of this shape if each rectangle is congruent and is 5 cm by 8 cm.

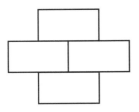

_____

4. Write the rule for the function represented by this table.

Input	Output
1	4
2	7
3	10
4	13
5	16

_____

5. If two angles of a triangle measure 50 degrees and 85 degrees, what is the measure of the third angle?

_____

Thursday ⟨14⟩

1. 90 ÷ 9 = _____

2. $8\overline{)1.008}$

3. What value of Z makes this equation true? (Remember the order of operations.)

$$5 \times Z + 3 = 23$$

_____

4. Draw a picture to show what $\frac{5}{4}$ means.

5. Meagan is taking piano and gymnastics lessons. She has a piano lesson every 7 days and a gymnastics lesson every 3 days. How often does she have both on the same day?

_____

Friday 〈14〉

Use the digits 1 through 9 to complete these number sentences. Use each digit only once. Are there any other possible solutions?

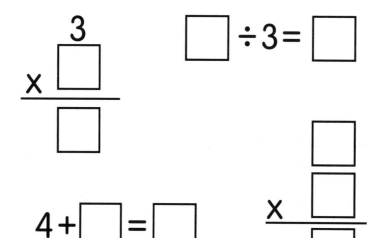

Daily Math Practice

Daily Progress Record 〈14〉

How many did you get correct each day? Color the squares.

	Monday	Tuesday	Wednesday	Thursday	Friday
5					
4					
3					
2					
1					

   EMC 755 • © Evan-Moor Corp.

1. 5.49 + 12.48 = _____

2. $\frac{5}{9}$
    $+\ \frac{1}{3}$

3. At lunchtime you have to choose one entree: pizza, a corn dog, or chili. You also have to choose one dessert: ice cream, fruit, or pie. How many possible entree/dessert combinations are there?

_____

4. What are the coordinates of the two points on this graph?

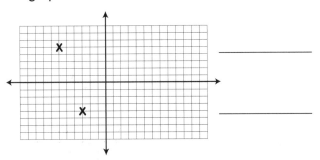

_____

_____

5. Sharon goes to two different grocery stores and compares the prices of candy bars. At Good Food Warehouse she can get 3 candy bars for 99¢. At Alpha Alpha, she can get 4 candy bars for $1.25. Which store has the better buy and why?

_____

_____

---

1. 12,300 − 26 = _____

2. $5\frac{1}{3}$
    $-\ 2\frac{2}{3}$

3. What place value does the 2 have in 1,386.972?

_____

4. Fill in the correct symbol.

< = >

⁻6 ◯ ⁺4

5. Use a factor tree to write the prime factorization of 72 using exponents.

Wednesday ⟨15⟩

1. $\frac{2}{3} \times \frac{1}{5} =$ _____

2. 1.26
   x 0.8

3. Name a pair of supplementary angles.

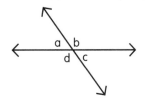

_____

4. Write this number in standard form.

   one hundred three and sixteen thousandths

   _____

5. Sheila and her sister Sarah are baby-sitting three kids for 5 hours. If the parents pay $2.50 per hour for each kid, how much will Sheila and Sarah each make?

   _____

Thursday ⟨15⟩

1. $0.49 \div 0.7 =$ _____

2. $15\overline{)1,230}$

3. How many faces does a triangular pyramid have?

   _____

4. What is the probability of getting a number less than 7 on a standard six-sided die?

   _____

5. A ball began to roll down a hill. It started at 1 foot per second, but the rate doubled each second after that. How fast will the ball be going in 10 seconds?

   _____

Friday ⟨15⟩

Here are the first 16 numbers in base ten:

1, 2, 3, 4, 5, 6, 7, 8, 9, 10, 11, 12, 13, 14, 15, 16

Here are the first 16 numbers in base four:

1, 2, 3, 10, 11, 12, 13, 20, 21, 22, 23, 30, 31, 32, 33, 100

What are the first 10 numbers in base three?

_____

Daily Progress Record ⟨15⟩

How many did you get correct each day? Color the squares.

	Monday	Tuesday	Wednesday	Thursday	Friday
5					
4					
3					
2					
1					

1. $5\frac{1}{4} + 1\frac{3}{4} =$ _____

2. $\frac{5}{8}$

   $+ \frac{1}{2}$

3. What is the volume of this cylinder? Remember: Volume is the area of the base multiplied by the height. Use 3.14 for π.

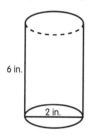

6 in.

2 in.

_____

4. Write this number in standard form.

   two thousand seven hundred and four tenths

   _____

5. Marla is saving to buy a new bicycle. The bicycle will cost her $250. She has saved $167.93 so far. How much more does she need?

   _____

Daily Math Practice **Tuesday** 16

1. $2 - 0.053 =$ _____

2. $6\frac{7}{8}$

   $- 2\frac{1}{4}$

3. What is the GCF of 12, 30, and 18?

   _____

4. Draw the other three parts of this shape, given that it has these two lines of symmetry.

5. Kayleen flips a coin and it lands on tails. She says that next time it will be heads for sure. Is Kayleen right or wrong? Explain your answer.

   _____

   _____

   _____

Wednesday ⬡16⬡

1. $\frac{4}{5} \times \frac{1}{3} =$ _____

2. $\begin{array}{r} 89 \\ \times\ 46 \\ \hline \end{array}$

3. Circle the letter of the figure that is congruent to the given white shape.

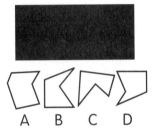

   A   B   C   D

4. What is 15 hours after 12:00 noon?

_____

5. Rosa is planting bulbs in her garden. She can plant 3 bulbs every 2 minutes. How long will it take her to plant 57 bulbs?

_____

Thursday ⬡16⬡

1. $\frac{3}{6} \div \frac{1}{2} =$ _____

2. $9\overline{)36}$

3. What are the next three numbers in this pattern?

10, 6, 18, 14, 26, 22, 34, ____, ____, ____

4. What shape is the label on a soup can if you cut straight up the label and peel it off the can?

_____

5. The temperature on a cold January morning fell from 29° to ⁻6°. How many degrees did the temperature fall?

_____

Pretend that a survey has been taken of the students in your class to find out their favorite TV shows. The graph represents this information. Label each section and make as many true statements as you can about your graph.

_____
_____
_____
_____
_____
_____
_____
_____

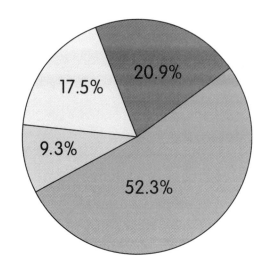

How many did you get correct each day? Color the squares.

	Monday	Tuesday	Wednesday	Thursday	Friday
5					
4					
3					
2					
1					

1. $0.36 + 12.9 =$ _____

2. $5\frac{7}{12}$
$+ \ 2\frac{11}{12}$
_____

3. How many minutes are in a day?

_____

4. All of these numbers are divisible by 3: 21, 33, 60, 45. Circle any of these numbers that are divisible by 3:

27   31   65   54

5. Teresa and Eva are walking home from school. They start out walking for 2 blocks and then running for 3 blocks and then repeating this pattern. If they walk 2 blocks in 4 minutes and run 3 blocks in 2 minutes, how long will it take them to go 18 blocks?

_____

---

1. $8\frac{1}{4} - 2\frac{3}{4} =$ _____

2. $\frac{11}{12}$
$- \ \frac{2}{3}$
_____

3. Which of these shapes tessellate?

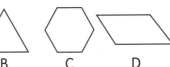

A   B   C   D

4. How many inches are in 15 yards?

_____

5. Dane is collecting stamps. He has 57 pages of stamps with an average of 30 stamps per page. If the average selling price of each stamp is 35¢, about how much are his stamps worth?

_____

Wednesday ⟨**17**⟩

1. $\frac{2}{3} \times \frac{1}{7} =$ _____

2. $3\frac{1}{2} \times 2\frac{3}{4} =$ _____

3. The associative property of addition allows one to say that $(3 + 2) + 4$ is the same as what?

_____

4. How many ounces are in 1 quart?
(1 quart = 4 cups and 1 cup = 8 ounces)

_____

5. Christy starts doing her homework at home. After every fifteen minutes of studying, she gets up and takes a five-minute stretch break. If she has 2 hours of homework to do, how long will it take her?

_____

Thursday ⟨**17**⟩

1. $3\frac{1}{2} \div 1\frac{1}{4} =$ _____

2. $5\overline{)1.26}$

3. What shape is every face of a pyramid except for the base?

_____

4. What is the LCM of 2, 3, and 5?

_____

5. Mateo's family took a trip to visit their relatives. If they drove for $2\frac{1}{2}$ hours at 55 mph, how many miles did they drive?

_____

Friday ⟨17⟩

What are the next two things in each of these patterns?

5, 8, 11, 14, 17, _____, _____

1, 1, 2, 3, 5, 8, _____, _____

2, 6, 18, 54, _____, _____

M, T, W, T, F, _____, _____

F, S, T, F, F, S, _____, _____

A, M, J, J, A, S, _____, _____

Daily Progress Record ⟨17⟩

How many did you get correct each day? Color the squares.

	Monday	Tuesday	Wednesday	Thursday	Friday
5					
4					
3					
2					
1					

1. $8\frac{5}{8} + \frac{3}{8} =$ _____

2. $\quad\frac{1}{4}$
    $+ \ \frac{1}{3}$
    _____

3. What is the probability of getting an 8 on a standard six-sided die?

    _____

4. Round the number 296,386,482 to the nearest million.

    _____

5. Your class collected this data. Construct an appropriate graph. Use a sheet of graph paper.

Month	Average Temperature
January	29
February	39
March	48
April	62
May	78

1. $10,000 - 29 =$ _____

2. $\quad 8\frac{1}{4}$
    $- \ 2\frac{1}{3}$
    _____

3. Give one good reason why 2,700 is NOT a good estimate for 903 times 29.

    _____

    _____

    _____

4. What is the measurement of the fourth angle of a quadrilateral if the others measure 80 degrees, 120 degrees, and 65 degrees?

    _____

5. Tara is playing her four CDs. The lengths of the four CDs are 45 minutes, 52 minutes, 38 minutes, and 47 minutes. If it takes her 2 minutes to change each CD, how long will it take to play all four CDs?

    _____

1. 0.26 x 0.18 = _____

2. $2\frac{4}{7} \times 1\frac{3}{5}$ = _____

3. Find the surface area of this figure.

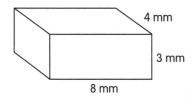

4 mm

3 mm

8 mm

_____

4. If Sachi, Sheryl, Sharon, Shannon, and Stephanie are all sitting in the back seat of the school bus, in how many different ways can they seat themselves?

_____

5. What three consecutive odd numbers have a sum of 45?

_____

---

1. $\frac{5}{8} \div \frac{2}{3}$ = _____

2. $2\overline{)5.27}$

3. If the mean of this data is 95, find the missing data.

103, 99, 90, 86, 105, 96, ___

4. Find the LCM of 3, 4, 6, and 8.

_____

5. Renee recently traveled with her family in their minivan. She sat in the back seat for the first half of the trip. Then she rode in the front seat for the next fourth of the trip, and then in the back seat for the last fourth. If the entire trip was 7 hours, how long did she ride in the front seat?

_____

Friday ⟨18⟩

If a rectangle has a perimeter of 24 centimeters, what are three possible sets of dimensions and the resulting areas?

	Length	Width	Area
1.	_____	_____	_____
2.	_____	_____	_____
3.	_____	_____	_____

Daily Progress Record ⟨18⟩

How many did you get correct each day? Color the squares.

	Monday	Tuesday	Wednesday	Thursday	Friday
5					
4					
3					
2					
1					

1. 256 + 384 = _____

2. 10,948
− 2,297
─────

3. If an equilateral triangle is reflected along one of its edges, what shape is created?

_____

4. What is the greatest fraction you can create using the digits 4, 7, and 9?

_____

5. A grocery store sells cans of mushrooms in three different sizes. This chart displays the prices of each. Which is the best buy?

Size	Price
8 oz.	$0.48
15 oz.	$0.85
22 oz.	$1.10

_____

1. Correct any mistakes or write "correct."

8 x 12 = 110 _____

2. Correct any mistakes or write "correct."

0.7 x 8 = 48 _____

3. List all the factors of 30.

_____

4. Name the first five prime numbers.

_____

5. Jim and his dad are building a straight fence. They put up 12 fence posts with 10 feet between each one. How long is their fence?

_____

1. Add one operational sign to make the equation true.

   1   3   6   5   9 = 195

2. Add a sign.

   5   2   1   0 = 520

3. How many ounces are in 6 pounds?

   _____

4. Which is larger, 0.08 or 0.028?

   _____

5. Wanda cut open a box that was in the shape of a rectangular prism. Which of these could NOT be a rectangular prism?

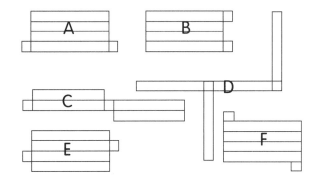

1. $\frac{1}{5} + \frac{1}{3} =$ _____

2. Write about how to solve this problem.

   3.5 – 0.9

   _____

   _____

   _____

3. When Joe got out of bed it was 58° in his room. He turned on the heater and it warmed up to 67°. How many degrees did the temperature rise?

   _____

4. On a die, the top and bottom numbers always add up to 7. What are the three pairs of numbers that each add up to 7?

   _____

5. If you only have a 3-quart pitcher and a 5-quart pitcher, how can you measure exactly 1 quart?

   _____

   _____

   _____

   _____

Friday 〈19〉

Jimmy is thinking of a number. He gives the following clues:

It is smaller than 100.
It is larger than 50.
It is not divisible by 5.
It is even.
It is divisible by 3.

Jimmy has not given us enough clues to find his number. List the numbers that Jimmy could be thinking of and then choose one of those numbers. Write a few more clues to help someone narrow in on the number you have selected.

_____

_____

_____

_____

Daily Progress Record 〈19〉

How many did you get correct each day? Color the squares.

	Monday	Tuesday	Wednesday	Thursday	Friday
5					
4					
3					
2					
1					

1. 29)324.8

2. 9,683
   x   12

3. Write 352.8 in word form.

   _____

4. Find the median of this data.

   14, 19, 26, 28, 18, 21, 30, 27

   _____

5. David is the president of his student council. When the leadership team met for the first time, he asked each person to shake everyone else's hand. If there were six people at this meeting, how many handshakes were made?

   _____

1. Correct any mistakes or write "correct."

   17 x 10 = 170 _____

2. Correct any mistakes or write "correct."

   5.3 – 0.7 = 5.4 _____

3. If two rectangles have the same area, must they have the same perimeter?

   _____

4. If two squares have the same area, must they have the same perimeter?

   _____

5. Colin is working to earn some money for a new CD player. On Saturday he earned half as much as he did on Sunday, but twice as much as he did on Friday. During those three days he earned $70. How much did he earn each day?

   _____

   _____

Wednesday 20

1. Add a sign.

1　9　6　2　1　8 = 109

2. Add a sign.

9　6　2　5　2　9 = 433

3. What place value does the 9 have in 290.846?

_____

4. Find the LCM of 8 and 9.

_____

5. Mariko walks into her dark bedroom to pull socks out of the dresser. If she has 5 pairs of white socks, 3 pairs of blue socks, and 4 pairs of pink socks that are single (not matched up), how many socks does she need to pull out to make sure that she ends up with 1 matching pair?

_____

Thursday 20

1. $9.5 \times 4.2 =$ _____

2. Write about how to solve this problem.

$8 \div 5$

_____

_____

_____

3. What comes next in this pattern?

5, 13, 21, 29, _____

4. What value would n have to make this a true equation?

$$16 = 4 \times n$$

_____

5. Jordan is rollerblading to his friend's house. His friend lives about 8 blocks away, and it takes Jordan about 20 seconds to rollerblade one block. About how long will it take Jordan to reach his friend's house?

_____

Friday ⟨20⟩

Landen's front lawn measures 20 feet by 8 feet. He counts to find that there are 120 blades of grass per square inch. How many blades of grass are in the entire lawn? Use proportions.

Do your work here.

Write your answer here.

Daily Progress Record ⟨20⟩

How many did you get correct each day? Color the squares.

	Monday	Tuesday	Wednesday	Thursday	Friday
5					
4					
3					
2					
1					

Monday ⟨21⟩

1. 120 x 27 = _____

2. $2\frac{1}{9}$
  $+ 3\frac{2}{3}$
  _____

3. What is the mode of this data?

35, 44, 42, 35, 44, 48, 27, 44, 49, 34

_____

4. What is the volume of a cube that is 6 cm on each edge?

_____

5. Determine the distance between the two points plotted on this coordinate system.

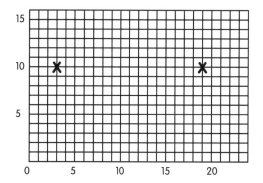

_____

Tuesday ⟨21⟩

1. Correct any mistakes or write "correct."

256 – 57 = 201 _____

2. Correct any mistakes or write "correct."

$\frac{1}{2} + \frac{1}{4} = \frac{2}{6}$ _____

3. What is 50% of 80?

_____

4. Fill in the correct symbol.

< = >

26.5 ◯ 25.89

5. Marissa is attempting to talk her parents into letting her have her own phone because she ties up the phone for so long each evening. She claims that she makes 15 calls every evening, each lasting an average of 6 minutes. One evening her parents wrote down the length of each call she made: 8, 4, 2, 7, 10, 5. Was Marissa's claim accurate?

_____

_____

1. Add a sign.

2   4   1   2 = 288

2. Add a sign.

9   6   2   5   8   0   7 = 8,818

3. Let $a = 3$ and $b = 2$.
What is the value of the expression $a \cdot b$?

_____

4. Circle the letter of the figure that is congruent to the given white shape.

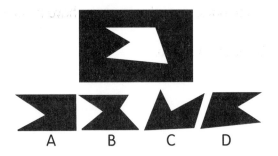

A   B   C   D

5. Shelley and Andre went hiking in the mountains. They climbed from an elevation of 8,540 feet to 9,885 feet. What was the difference in elevation that they climbed?

_____

1. $\frac{1}{2} - \frac{1}{5} =$ _____

2. Write about how to solve this problem.

14 x 26

_____

_____

_____

3. How many minutes are in 2 hours and 15 minutes?

_____

4. What is 12% of 125?

_____

5. Glenn is collecting aluminum cans to earn money. He has 5 bags that hold an average of 300 cans each. If he gets $2.00 for every 450 cans, about how much money will he get?

_____

    EMC 755 • © Evan-Moor Corp.

Friday ⟨21⟩

Charles has been assigned several chores around the house. He washes the supper dishes every fifth day, he takes out the trash every other day, and he vacuums the house every seven days. How often does he have to do all three things on the same day?

Do your work here.

Write your answer here.

Daily Progress Record ⟨21⟩

How many did you get correct each day? Color the squares.

	Monday	Tuesday	Wednesday	Thursday	Friday
5					
4					
3					
2					
1					

1. $\frac{1}{3} \div \frac{1}{3} =$ _____

2. $\begin{array}{r} 0.5 \\ \times\ 0.6 \\ \hline \end{array}$

3. If the temperature outside is ⁻5, what does the negative sign mean?

_____

_____

4. Write the rule for the function represented by this table.

Input	Output
1	5
2	10
3	15
4	20
5	25

_____

5. Isaac and Juanita are collecting apples to make an apple pie. Isaac picks up 3 apples every minute and Juanita picks up 5 apples every two minutes. If they need 40 apples for a pie, about how long will it take both of them to collect enough apples?

_____

---

1. Correct any mistakes or write "correct."

   $\frac{5}{6} \div \frac{1}{3} = 2\frac{1}{2}$ _____

2. Correct any mistakes or write "correct."

   $0.3 \times 0.2 = 0.6$ _____

3. Draw the next two figures in this pattern.

   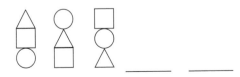 _____ _____

4. How many sides does a hexagon have?

   _____

5. Monique is jumping rope and jumps 3 times every 5 seconds. About how long does it take her to jump 100 times?

   _____

   EMC 755 • © Evan-Moor Corp.

Wednesday ⟨22⟩

1. Add a sign.

6   6   5   2   5 = 26.6

2. Add a sign.

9   7   8   8   4   2 = 1,820

3. The commutative property of multiplication says that 5 x 2 is the same as what?

_____

4. How many grams are in 2 kilograms?

_____

5. Joseph and Chandra are cleaning their house, which has 12 rooms, each about the same size. If Joseph cleans them by himself, it takes him 6 hours. If Chandra cleans them by herself, it takes her 12 hours. If they both clean the house, they will finish in 4 hours. If they work together, how many rooms will Chandra clean and how many will Joseph clean?

_____

_____

Thursday ⟨22⟩

1. 16% of 40 is _____

2. ⁻7 – 2 = _____

3. Draw three different acute angles.

4. Name the ordered pair for each of the points marked.

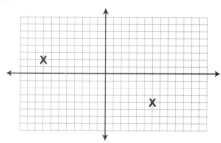

_____   _____

5. Lexi and Gina are planting a garden. They have planted six rows and plan to plant four more rows. Each row is 8 feet long. If the rows were end to end, how long would they be?

_____

Friday ⟨22⟩

Fill in the boxes on this square using the numbers 1 through 9. You may use each number only once. The goal is to have each row, column, and diagonal add up to the same sum. Explain the strategies you used to solve this problem.

Daily Progress Record ⟨22⟩

How many did you get correct each day? Color the squares.

	Monday	Tuesday	Wednesday	Thursday	Friday
5					
4					
3					
2					
1					

Monday ⟨23⟩

1. 2.9 + 0.26 = _____

2. $5\frac{1}{3}$
   $- 2\frac{1}{4}$

3. Write 826 in word form.

   _____

4. Estimate 398 x 51.

   _____

5. Pierre has 11 coins that total 82¢. What are the coins?

   _____

   _____

Tuesday ⟨23⟩

1. Correct any mistakes or write "correct."

   2.5 + 3.8 = 6.3 _____

2. Correct any mistakes or write "correct."

   $2\frac{1}{2} + 3\frac{1}{2} = 6$ _____

3. List all the factors of 25. Circle the prime factors.

   _____

4. How many edges does a sphere have?

   _____

5. Garth collects postcards from around the world and decides to organize them. He puts them into an album that holds 480 postcards. He fills two albums and one-fourth of another album. How many postcards does he have?

   _____

Wednesday ⟨23⟩

1. Add a sign.

6   3   2   8 = 79

2. Add a sign.

4   5   6   9 = 4,104

3. It's 12°F outside and the temperature drops 18 degrees overnight. What's the temperature in the morning?

_____

4. Name three letters of the alphabet that have one and only one line of symmetry.

_____

5. How many blocks are in this structure? _____ Does this structure have the same or a different view when you look at it from each of the four corners?

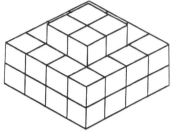

_____

Thursday ⟨23⟩

1. $\frac{1}{2} \div \frac{2}{3} =$ _____

2. Write about how to solve this problem.

9 – 0.6

_____

_____

3. Find the mean, median, and mode of these test scores:

95, 88, 79, 92, 78, 88, 88, 93, 100, 69, 98

_____   _____   _____

4. What is the range for the data in problem 3?

_____

5. If five friends buy a package of 38 balloons, how should they divide them?

_____

_____

Friday ⟨23⟩

Use the following clues to determine what number goes in each labeled region of this figure and what color each region should be. Write your answers on the grid below.

1. F is purple and its number is higher than A.
2. One of the colors is red.
3. The sum of the numbers in the square is 7, the sum of the numbers in the large triangle is 9, and the sum of the numbers in the circle is 12.
4. The brown region is even and the green region is odd.
5. The blue and orange regions add up to 5.
6. The region that is contained in all three shapes is red.
7. Brown is 4 and red is 1 OR brown is 1 and red is 4.
8. Green is less than purple.
9. The blue region is in the circle and square, but not in the triangle.
10. Orange is 3.
11. E is 1.

Region	Number	Color
A		
B		
C		
D		
E		
F		

Daily Progress Record ⟨23⟩

How many did you get correct each day? Color the squares.

	Monday	Tuesday	Wednesday	Thursday	Friday
5					
4					
3					
2					
1					

1. $\frac{3}{4} \times \frac{3}{5} =$ _____

2.
$$\begin{array}{r} 5.2 \\ -\ 0.26 \\ \hline \end{array}$$

3. Estimate the area of this shape.

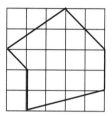

_____

4. What is 20% of 40?

_____

5. Susan is 18 years younger than her mom. Her mom is 3 years younger than Susan's dad. If Susan's dad is 41, how old is Susan?

_____

1. Correct any mistakes or write "correct."

   $25^2 = 625$ _____

2. Correct any mistakes or write "correct."

   $1\frac{1}{3} \times 3 = 3\frac{1}{3}$ _____

3. What place value does the 3 have in 4.97532?

_____

4. Evaluate the expression $3 \times a \times b$, if $a = 1$ and $b = 5$.

_____

5. Roxie is typing a report on the kiwi bird from New Zealand. The report turns out to be about 5 pages. On each page there are approximately 18 lines with 15 words in each line. About how many words are in the report?

_____

EMC 755 • © Evan-Moor Corp.

Wednesday ⬡24

1. Add a sign.

   5   5   2   6   5   8 = 1,210

2. Add a sign.

   9   9   6   3   5 = 961

3. How many angles are on the interior of any octagon?

   _____

4. Find the mean of these test scores.

   95, 88, 79, 92, 76, 85, 88, 91, 100, 89

   _____

5. Joel is saving to buy a new stereo system for his bedroom. The stereo costs $190 and the set of speakers costs $180. He has saved $350 so far. Does he have enough to buy the stereo system yet? Explain why or why not.

   _____

   _____

   _____

Thursday ⬡24

1. $\frac{4}{5} + \frac{4}{7} =$ _____

2. Write about how to solve this problem.

   $$10 \div 3$$

   _____

   _____

   _____

3. How many feet are in 4 miles?

   _____

4. How many different ways can you arrange four pictures on a wall if you want them in a straight line horizontally?

   _____

5. Susie is planting a circular flower bed with a radius of $3\frac{1}{2}$ feet. She plans to surround it with wire fencing that costs $0.89 a foot. How much does Susie need to spend on fencing?

   _____

Friday ⟨24⟩

Van Air has recently released a new CD that is quickly becoming very popular. Here is a chart showing how many CDs have sold each week.

Week	Number of CDs Sold
1	121
2	153
3	190
4	224
5	245

If sales continue at a similar rate, predict how many CDs you think will sell during week 6 and explain why.

_____

_____

_____

Daily Progress Record ⟨24⟩

How many did you get correct each day? Color the squares.

	Monday	Tuesday	Wednesday	Thursday	Friday
5					
4					
3					
2					
1					

1. $^-12 \times 27 =$ _____

2. $\frac{5}{7}$
   $+ \frac{2}{3}$

3. What value for *s* would make this equation true?

   $$4 + s = 25$$

   _____

4. What is any number multiplied by zero?

   _____

5. On field day, Scott School had a tug of war with a rope. One side had twice as many kids as the other side. The side with fewer kids had 3 adults helping out, which made a total of 15 people on that side. How many kids were on the other side?

   _____

1. Correct any mistakes or write "correct."

   $1.2 \div 0.6 = 2.0$ _____

2. Correct any mistakes or write "correct."

   $126 - 99 = 25$ _____

3. Write this number in standard form.

   seven thousand twenty-six

   _____

4. Round 97,489 to the nearest thousand.

   _____

5. Barry is in a pie-eating contest. He claims that he can eat a pie that is divided into six equal pieces in 2 minutes. If he is going to eat the whole pie in 2 minutes, how long does he have to eat each piece?

   _____

1. Add a sign.

2   6   9   1   2 = 23,712

2. Add a sign.

4   6   3   2   8 = 579

3. What are all the common factors of 6 and 8?

_____

4. How many quarts are in 8 gallons?

_____

5. A country's flag has three horizontal stripes: one red, one blue, and one green. How many different ways can the colors be arranged on the flag?

_____

1. $9.2 \div 2 =$ _____

2. Write about how to solve this problem.

12 x 49

_____

_____

_____

3. What is the perimeter of a rectangle that is 4 feet by 6 feet?

_____

4. What is the mode of this data?

25, 33, 30, 27, 35, 33

_____

5. Ben is sailing on a ship. The ship goes 600 miles north and then turns west. It travels 200 miles west and then turns south for 450 miles. It turns west again and travels 170 miles and turns south once more and travels 150 miles. Where has the ship ended up in relation to where it started?

_____

   EMC 755 • © Evan-Moor Corp.

Draw how this building would look if you stood on the opposite corner, looking down on the building from the north rather than from the south.

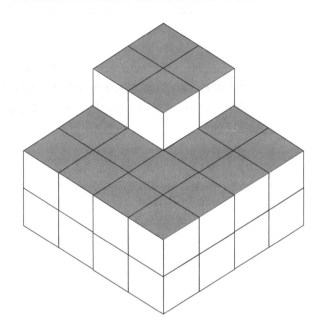

Daily Progress Record 〈25〉

How many did you get correct each day? Color the squares.

	Monday	Tuesday	Wednesday	Thursday	Friday
5					
4					
3					
2					
1					

Monday ⟨26⟩

1. $90 \div \frac{1}{9} =$ _____

2. What is the median of these test scores?

   95, 88, 79, 92, 76, 85, 88, 91, 100, 67, 98

   _____

3. What is the range of the test scores in problem 2?

   _____

4. Use a factor tree to write the prime factorization of 54. Then write the result using exponents.

5. Jamila has a bag that contains one tile for each letter of the alphabet. What is the probability that she will pull out a vowel?

   If another bag has 52 tiles in it with the same percentage of vowels and consonants as above, how many vowels are there in it?

   _____

Tuesday ⟨26⟩

1. Correct any mistakes or write "correct."

   $2\frac{1}{3} - \frac{2}{3} = 1\frac{1}{3}$ _____

2. Correct any mistakes or write "correct."

   $49 \div 0.7 = 7$ _____

3. What are the next two numbers in this pattern?

   1, 4, 13, 40, 121, _____, _____

4. What value of x makes this a true sentence?

   $5 \cdot x = 75$

   _____

5. Patrick was outside riding his horse one morning when he noticed that the fence posts needed to be painted around the corral. The rectangular corral is 50 feet by 30 feet and the fence posts are spaced 5 feet apart. How many fence posts does Patrick need to paint?

   _____

                                        EMC 755 • © Evan-Moor Corp.

1. Add a sign.

9   8   7   1   1   1 = 876

2. Add a sign.

1   2   6   5 = 25.2

3. Given this isosceles triangle, which two angles are congruent?

_____

4. What is the volume of a rectangular prism that is 6 cm by 3 cm by 2 cm?

_____

5. A balance scale is perfectly balanced with 2 cans of soda on one side and 1 can of soda and 8 ounces of sand on the other. How much does each can of soda weigh?

_____

Daily Math Practice **Thursday** ⟨26⟩

1. $25 - (^-9) =$ _____

2. Write about how to solve this problem.

0.5×0.2

_____

_____

_____

3. What is the LCM of 3, 7, and 8?

_____

4. Kareem says that $(3 + 2) + 6 = 3 + (2 + 6)$, where you add what is inside the parentheses first. Kareem is correct. What property is he using?

_____

5. Else's dad is a policeman. One afternoon her dad stopped 19 people for speeding. This was 12 more than the previous day and 7 more than each of the prior two days combined. How many people did Else's dad stop for speeding over those three days?

_____

Trevor built the bookshelf shown below. Each shelf is 2 feet by 2 feet, and the bookshelf is 4 feet tall with a solid board across the back. If Trevor wants to paint all surfaces, including the undersides of each shelf and both sides of the backboard, how many square feet will he paint?

_____

If each can of spray paint paints 25 square feet, how many cans of paint will he need? Use proportions to solve the problem.

_____

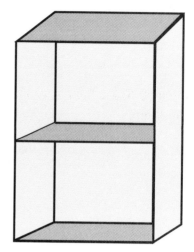

How many did you get correct each day? Color the squares.

	Monday	Tuesday	Wednesday	Thursday	Friday
5					
4					
3					
2					
1					

1. $2.5 \div 0.5 =$ _____

2. $1\frac{1}{2} \times 2\frac{1}{4} =$ _____

3. List three numbers that are less than 3 and greater than 2.

_____

4. List the first five composite numbers.

_____

5. City Park was receiving lots of rain. It rained 11 inches in five and one-half hours. What was the average rainfall for one hour?

_____

1. Correct any mistakes or write "correct."

$\frac{1}{8} \times \frac{4}{5} = \frac{1}{10}$ _____

2. Correct any mistakes or write "correct."

$25 - 1.3 = 1.2$ _____

3. What is 6 less than 2?

_____

4. If the rule for this table is to add 2 and then multiply by 3, complete the table.

Input	Output
1	
2	12
5	
8	30
	42

5. Shirley has a bottle that is half full. She pours it into another bottle and it fills that bottle one-third full. If the second bottle holds 2 quarts, how much does the first bottle hold?

_____

Wednesday 27

1. Add a sign.

1   2   9   6   4 = 976

2. Add a sign.

8   6   5   5 = 173

3. Estimate 52 x 197.

_____

4. List at least three numerals that have one or more lines of symmetry.

_____

5. Mark is traveling by bus and needs to go from Denver to San Diego and then on to San Francisco. The charge from Denver to San Diego is $17.50 and the charge from San Diego to San Francisco is $8.75. How much will the ride cost?

_____

Thursday 27

1. $\frac{5}{6} - \frac{1}{3} =$ _____

2. Write about how to solve this problem.

$12 \div 7$

_____

_____

_____

3. What are angles that measure more than 90 degrees called?

_____

4. When April was born, she weighed 8 pounds, 9 ounces. If her weight doubled in the first six months, what was her weight after six months?

_____

5. Kiyoko spends Saturdays collecting aluminum cans. The grocery store pays her 25¢ a pound for the cans, and they estimate that 35 cans weigh a pound. About how many cans does Kiyoko need to collect to earn $1.50?

_____

Friday ⟨27⟩

Becky just got a new bicycle. Describe all the geometric shapes or concepts that you see on this bicycle.

_____

_____

_____

_____

Daily Math Practice

Daily Progress Record ⟨27⟩

How many did you get correct each day? Color the squares.

	Monday	Tuesday	Wednesday	Thursday	Friday
5					
4					
3					
2					
1					

1. $5\frac{1}{2} - 3\frac{3}{4} =$ _____

2.
```
   15.2
 +  9.83
```

3. What is the GCF of 2, 5, and 6?

_____

4. What three symbols come next in this pattern?

 ____ ____ ____

5. Heidi's family is trying to decide on the shorter of two routes for a trip from Georgetown to Cypress City. One route begins in Georgetown and goes 53 miles to Cycle City, then 28 miles to Aspen and 98 miles to Cypress City. The second route also begins in Georgetown and goes 28 miles to Canon City, then 49 miles to Grover and 85 miles to Cypress City. Which route is shorter and by how much?

_____

---

1. Correct any mistakes or write "correct."

$\frac{1}{4} \div \frac{1}{2} = \frac{1}{2}$ _____

2. Correct any mistakes or write "correct."

1,496 + 14,692 = 16,188 _____

3. Vic is part of a relay team with three other runners. If each person runs 3,100 yards, about how many miles long is the race?

_____

4. In how many different ways can you arrange the digits 1 through 3?

_____

5. What is the difference between the largest region and the smallest region on this graph?

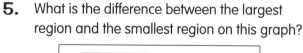

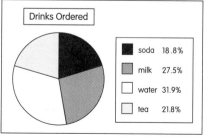

Drinks Ordered

soda 18.8%
milk 27.5%
water 31.9%
tea 21.8%

_____

Wednesday ⟨28⟩

1. Add a sign.

3   2   5   8   6   2 = 1,187

2. Add a sign.

4   9   6   5   9   8 = 6,647

3. A can of soup is a representation of what 3-D shape?

If the area of the base is 4 square inches and the can is 5 inches tall, what is the volume?

Remember: Volume is the area of the base multiplied by the height.

_____

4. What is 19 degrees higher than 62°?

_____

5. Sarah drank 75% of the soda out of a 12-ounce can. How many ounces are left in the can?

_____

Thursday ⟨28⟩

1. $6,756 \div 9.7 =$ _____

2. Write about how to solve this problem.

$$1\frac{1}{2} \times 3\frac{1}{3}$$

_____

_____

_____

3. If $x = 2$, what is the value of this expression?

$$2 \cdot x + 3$$

_____

4. The mean of this data is 8. What two numbers could go in the blanks?

12, 4, 9, 13, 7, 11, 5, 2, ____, ____

5. As Doug and his dog walk the neighborhood during the summertime, bats swoop down to eat the bugs flying in the light of the streetlights. He sees 3 bats at every streetlight, and there are streetlights at every intersection and one in the middle of each block. If Doug walks 10 blocks, how many bats will he see?

_____

Friday 28

The grid below represents the blocks of the city George lives in. Start at the **X** and follow these directions:

Travel north 4 blocks and turn left.
Go 8 blocks and turn south.
Go south 3 blocks and then turn right.
After going 2 blocks, turn right again
and go 5 blocks to the museum.

What is the ordered pair of the museum?

_____

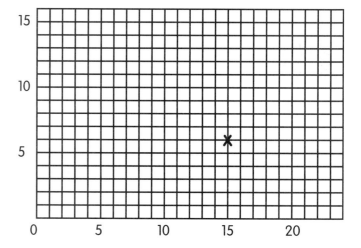

Daily Math Practice

Daily Progress Record 28

How many did you get correct each day? Color the squares.

	Monday	Tuesday	Wednesday	Thursday	Friday
5					
4					
3					
2					
1					

EMC 755 • © Evan-Moor Corp.

1. 0.5 × 2.1 = _____

2.   109,283
       + 905,861

3. Given the number 256.398, what digit is in the tenths place?

_____

4. Construct a graph for this information. Use a sheet of graph paper.

Month	Number of Students' Birthdays
January	12
February	14
March	20
April	16
May	10
June	12

5. Alex has a pet snake that eats 1 mouse every week. How many mice will the snake eat if Alex has the snake for 4 years?

_____

 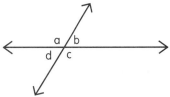
1. Correct any mistakes or write "correct."

56 ÷ 8 = 6 _____

2. Correct any mistakes or write "correct."

2.4 + 0.13 = 3.7 _____

3. Round 378,903.97 to the nearest hundred thousand.

_____

4. Name two pairs of adjacent angles.

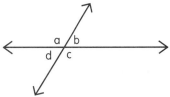

_____

5. Julia bought 300 pounds of grain for her horses. When a heavy rain flooded the storage shed, 30% of the grain rotted and had to be thrown out. How many pounds of grain will she be able to use?

_____

1. Add a sign.

7   3   3   5   1   5 = 489

2. Add a sign.

2   6   8   2 = 2,132

3. What shape has 10 sides?

_____

4. What is the perimeter of a triangle whose sides measure 15 cm, 17 cm, and 10 cm?

_____

5. If we add the ages of Jim, his father, and his grandfather, we get 137. The grandfather is 70 years older than Jim, and Jim is 31 years younger than his father. How old are each of these three people?

_____

_____

_____

1. 0.35 + 5.2 = _____

2. Write about how to solve this problem.

$$1\frac{2}{5} \div 2\frac{1}{4}$$

_____

_____

_____

3. What is the LCM of 3 and 5?

_____

4. What is the area of a rectangle that is 2.4 inches by 0.5 inches?

_____

5. How many triangles are in this robot's face?

_____

Hobby Shop is selling model cars and model trucks for 50% off this week. At the sale price, you can buy one car and one truck for $13.00. Also at the sale price, you can buy 4 trucks and 2 cars for $42.00. What is the sale price and the original price of the model car and the model truck?

_____

_____

Daily Math Practice

Daily Progress Record 29

How many did you get correct each day? Color the squares.

	Monday	Tuesday	Wednesday	Thursday	Friday
5					
4					
3					
2					
1					

1. $\frac{2}{5} \div \frac{5}{9} =$ _____

2. $\begin{array}{r} 9.26 \\ -4.3 \\ \hline \end{array}$

3. What time is 60 hours after 3:00 A.M.?

_____

4. What is the measurement of the third angle of a triangle if the first two angles measure 63 degrees and 87 degrees?

_____

5. Carlos estimated an answer to be 500, while Julie's estimate for the same problem was 450. Could both estimates be right? Explain why or why not.

_____

_____

_____

---

1. Correct any mistakes or write "correct."

$\frac{1}{3} \div \frac{1}{2} = \frac{3}{2}$ _____

2. Correct any mistakes or write "correct."

$0.5 \times 0.1 = 0.5$ _____

3. What is the range of this data?

31, 35, 29, 27, 31, 29, 33, 31, 19

_____

4. What is the probability of getting a 1 or a 6 on a standard six-sided die? If you were to roll the die 60 times, how many times would you expect to get a 1 or a 6?

_____

5. Write four math sentences that have an answer of 2.4. Use a different operation in each sentence.

_____

_____

_____

_____

1. Add a sign.

4 9 6 1 8 9 = 307

2. Add a sign.

2 4 9 6 = 992

3. What value of m makes this a true number sentence?

$m + 3 + m = 3$

_____

4. What number comes next in this pattern?

41, 39, 40, 38, 39, 37, 38, _____

5. How many blocks are needed to build this structure?

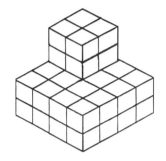

_____

---

1. $(^-4) + (^-2) =$ _____

2. Write about how to solve this problem.

59×27

_____

_____

_____

3. The median of this data is 16. What is the value for the blank?

12, 17, 16, 19, 8, _____

4. How many feet are in 17 yards?

_____

5. Liam and Lydia have been saving money to buy their parents a present. Liam has saved $5.28 and Lydia has saved $8.86. The present they want to buy will cost $24.75. How much more do Liam and Lydia need to save?

_____

Friday 30

Liz and Josh are both runners. One day they came to school bragging about how far they had run over the weekend. Liz said that she had run 4 miles and Josh said that he had run 6,000 yards. Please settle their dispute by writing about who ran farther and why. (Remember, there are 5,280 feet in a mile.) Use proportions to solve the problem.

_____

_____

_____

_____

Daily Progress Record ⬡ 30

How many did you get correct each day? Color the squares.

	Monday	Tuesday	Wednesday	Thursday	Friday
5					
4					
3					
2					
1					

EMC 755 · © Evan-Moor Corp.

1. 2.52 ÷ 8 = _____

2.   591
   x 26

3. What is the best estimate of the height of a textbook: 7 cm, 27 cm, or 52 cm?

_____

4. What is the smallest fraction you can write using each of the digits 4, 8, and 9?

_____

5. Sean is one-fourth his dad's height. If his dad is 6 feet, 6 inches tall, how tall is Sean?

_____

1. Correct any mistakes or write "correct."

$2\frac{1}{2} - 1\frac{1}{2} = 1$ _____

2. Correct any mistakes or write "correct."

1,964 + 2,043 = 3,907_____

3. How many cups are in 2 quarts?

_____

4. Write 258 in word form.

_____

5. If you have spinner A and your friend has spinner B, who has the best chance of getting a higher total after 5 spins?

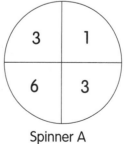   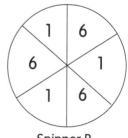

Spinner A   Spinner B

_____

1. Add a sign.

1 1 3 0 2 5 = 45.2

2. Add a sign.

9 0 0 0 1 0 0 = 90

3. What is the volume of a triangular prism that is 6 inches high with a base area of 12 square inches? Remember: Volume is the area of the base multiplied by the height.

_____

4. The identity property of multiplication says that anything times 1 is always what?

_____

5. Brandy went to a fantastic parade and saw 12 bands. If each band had an average of 120 members, about how many band members did she see during the parade?

_____

1. $5\frac{1}{2} + 2\frac{1}{3} =$ _____

2. Write about how to solve this problem.

3 – (⁻4)

_____

_____

_____

3. Fill in the correct symbol.

< = >

5 ◯ ⁻8

4. Circle the letter of the shape that is congruent to the first shape.

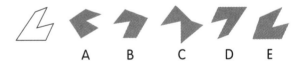

A   B   C   D   E

5. Herman is half as old as his sister. In seven years he will be two-thirds his sister's age. How old is Herman currently?

_____

Friday ⟨31⟩

Celina is making squares with toothpicks. She notices that in making one square, she uses 4 toothpicks. She continues the pattern and notices that it takes 7 toothpicks to build two squares side by side. To build three squares in a line, she will need 10 toothpicks. If she continues this pattern, how many toothpicks will she need to make 90 squares in a straight line?

_____

How many squares can she build in this pattern if the box she has contains 1,000 toothpicks?

_____

Explain how you figured out one of these answers.

_____

_____

_____

Daily Progress Record ⟨31⟩

How many did you get correct each day? Color the squares.

	Monday	Tuesday	Wednesday	Thursday	Friday
5					
4					
3					
2					
1					

Monday ⟨32⟩

1. $483\overline{)67,716.6}$

2. $\begin{array}{r} (^-5) \\ + \ (^-8) \\ \hline \end{array}$

3. If $s = 5$, what value does s^2 have?

_____

4. Use the line drawn as a line of symmetry. Reflect the word HELLO and write it on the other side of the line of symmetry.

HELLO |

5. The sum of Leda's age and Ginger's age is 15. Write an equation stating this. The product of their ages is 56. Write an equation stating this. If Leda is older than Ginger, how old is each girl?

_____

_____

_____

Tuesday ⟨32⟩

1. Correct any mistakes or write "correct."

   $6 \times 8 = 56$ _____

2. Correct any mistakes or write "correct."

   $5.6 + 1.63 = 7.23$ _____

3. List eight numbers that would have a mode of 6.

   _____

4. Find the area of this quadrilateral.

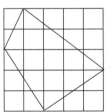

_____

5. What time is it when someone says twenty-three hundred?

_____

EMC 755 • © Evan-Moor Corp.

1. Add a sign.

4   6   9   2   5   2 = 4,744

2. Add a sign.

4   6   2   1   8 = 8,316

3. In how many different orders can Eli play 4 CDs?

_____

4. What is the perimeter of this shape?

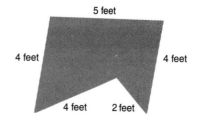

5 feet

4 feet   4 feet

4 feet   2 feet

_____

5. If Namid has 8 coins that total 68¢, what are the coins?

_____

_____

---

1. (⁻4) + (⁻7) = _____

2. Write about how to solve this problem.

(⁻8) − (⁻2)

_____

_____

_____

3. Round 390,358 to the nearest thousand.

_____

4. List all the factors of 18. Circle the prime factors.

_____

5. Emily and Holly are collecting dolls. They have 39 dolls between them. Write an equation showing this. Emily has 7 fewer than Holly. Write an equation showing this. How many dolls does each girl have?

_____

_____

_____

Friday 〈32〉

Mentally compute the following product (without a calculator and without figuring it out the traditional way). After you have the answer, write down the steps that you mentally went through to find this product.

What is 49 x 19? _____

_____

_____

_____

_____

Daily Math Practice

Daily Progress Record 〈32〉

How many did you get correct each day? Color the squares.

	Monday	Tuesday	Wednesday	Thursday	Friday
5					
4					
3					
2					
1					

Monday ⟨33⟩

1. $(^-4) + (^-3) =$ _____

2. $\begin{array}{r} (^-5) \\ + \quad 9 \\ \hline \end{array}$

3. What temperature in Fahrenheit is 28 degrees below freezing?

_____

4. Which weighs more, 1 gram or 1 pound?

_____

5. There are four houses on a block that is in the shape of a square. If you wanted to make paths that connected all four houses with each of the others, how many paths would you have to make?

_____

Tuesday ⟨33⟩

1. Correct any mistakes or write "correct."

$(^-4) + (^-2) = (^-6)$ _____

2. Correct any mistakes or write "correct."

$2\frac{1}{5} + 3\frac{2}{3} = 5\frac{3}{8}$ _____

3. What shape is the base of a cylinder?

_____

4. How many degrees are in a straight angle?

_____

5. If you fold up this shape it will make a cube. What number will be opposite the 6?

_____

	1	
2	3	
	4	5
		6

1. Add a sign.

4   5   6   9   2 = 364

2. Add a sign.

9   1   4   5   5 = 0.2

3. Graph the points (-3, 5) and (8, -2) on this coordinate grid.

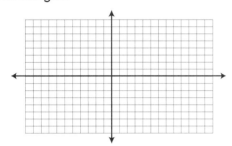

4. What is the rule used for this function table?

Input	1	2	3	4	5
Output	-3	-2	-1	0	1

_____

5. Pedro is playing video games. He is getting pretty good at Driving Max and can move up a level in an average of 8 minutes. If he plays for 3 hours straight, starting on level 9, on what level will he finish?

_____

---

1.   4,376
      x   253

2. Write about how to solve this problem.

$$5\frac{2}{7} - 1\frac{1}{2}$$

_____

_____

_____

3. In the number 367.4973, what digit is in the tens place?

_____

4. List the first three multiples of 6.

_____

5. In football, a team can score points in these ways:

Type of Play	Number of Points
Touchdown	6
Field goal	3
Safety	2
Conversion after touchdown	2
Extra kick after touchdown	1

A touchdown must be made in order to attempt either of the last two plays. Given this information, in how many ways can a team score 10 points?

_____

Friday ⟨33⟩

What could this graph be representing? Title the graph and label each axis. Create a legend for the graph. After you have done this, make as many statements and/or inferences as you can about the graph. Use a sheet of paper if necessary.

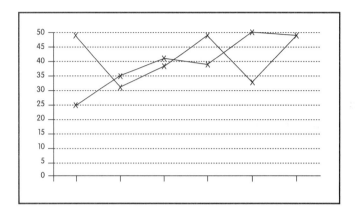

Daily Progress Record ⟨33⟩

How many did you get correct each day? Color the squares.

	Monday	Tuesday	Wednesday	Thursday	Friday
5					
4					
3					
2					
1					

1. $4 - (^-2) = $ _____

2. $5\frac{1}{5}$
$+ 2\frac{3}{4}$

3. Estimate the answer to $19.3 - 7.5$.

_____

4. What are the next three numbers in this pattern?

4, 20, 100, 500, _____, _____, _____

5. In any given 60 minutes, how many times will the two hands on a clock form right angles?

_____

1. Correct any mistakes or write "correct."

$6 - (^-4) = 10$ _____

2. Correct any mistakes or write "correct."

$64 \div 0.8 = 8$ _____

3. What polygon has 5 sides?

_____

4. What is the value of x in this equation?
$5x + 3 = 23$

_____

5. The Chungs are going on a vacation to California. They have three amusement parks to choose from: Sea World, Disneyland, and Knott's Berry Farm. They have three beaches to choose from: Huntington, Balboa, and Venice. In addition, they have two restaurants to choose from: The Cheesecake Factory or the Tail of the Whale. How many different combinations do the Chungs have to choose from when selecting an amusement park, a beach, and a restaurant?

_____

EMC 755 • © Evan-Moor Corp.

1. Add a sign.

7   6   2   1   0 = 752

2. Add a sign.

9   0   0   3   0 = 30

3. Name a pair of vertical angles.

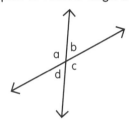

4. A rectangular prism has a base with an area of 15 square meters. If the height is 2 meters, what is the volume?

_____

5. There are 18 animals on the Harrys' farm. Some are emus (two-legged) and some are alpacas (four-legged). If there are 60 legs touching the ground, how many of each animal are there?

_____

1. (⁻6) + 8 = _____

2. Write about how to solve this problem.

0.35 x 0.9

_____

_____

_____

3. Dustin is selling pencils. He sells 10 pencils for $1.50 or 3 pencils for 40¢. Which is the better buy?

_____

4. Write this number in standard form.

six hundred fifty-three and five tenths

_____

5. The average of 5 numbers is 90. If the first four numbers are 85, 92, 89, and 95, what is the fifth number?

_____

Friday ⬡34

Use the following clues to determine what number goes in each labeled region of this figure and what color each region should be. Write your answers on the grid.

1. The numbers are all between 0 and 10, and no number is used more than once.
2. The purple region is 5.
3. The product of the regions in the triangle is 48. The sum of these regions is 15.
4. The numbers 2 and 7 are not used.
5. The blue region is only in the triangle.
6. A and G add up to 7.
7. Brown, purple, and orange are in the circle.
8. 8 is in all three shapes.
9. Brown is in the circle and rectangle, but not in the triangle.
10. C is the largest number.
11. Green and pink are in the rectangle only.
12. 1 is in the yellow region.
13. A is smaller than G.
14. Either A is green or F is yellow.

Region	Number	Color
A		
B		
C		
D		
E		
F		
G		

Daily Progress Record ⬡34

How many did you get correct each day? Color the squares.

	Monday	Tuesday	Wednesday	Thursday	Friday
5					
4					
3					
2					
1					

Monday ⟨35⟩

1. $\frac{2}{7} \div \frac{7}{9} =$ _____

2.   1.35
   x 0.29

3. Write the rule for the function represented by this table.

Input	Output
1	1
2	3
3	5
4	7
5	9

_____

4. Three consecutive numbers add up to 369. What are the three numbers?

_____

5. Kurt is buying stamps. How many 3¢ stamps are in a book of a dozen stamps?

_____

Tuesday ⟨35⟩

1. Correct any mistakes or write "correct."

$\frac{1}{3} \times \frac{3}{4} = \frac{1}{4}$ _____

2. Correct any mistakes or write "correct."

$8 - (^-2) = 6$ _____

3. Round 358,353,978 to the nearest million.

_____

4. Find the GCF of 20 and 16.

_____

5. Randy bought three items at the store. He bought a CD for $14.95, a video tape for $3.99, and a set of headphones for $19.98. What was his total?

_____

Wednesday ⟨35⟩

1. Add a sign.

4   7   1   0   3 = 4,841

2. Add a sign.

1   7   9   6   2   9   3 = 18,055

3. What three-dimensional shape has no faces?

_____

4. Find the perimeter of this shape.

6 feet
6 feet
3 feet
6 feet
6 feet
3 feet

_____

5. Amber is walking down the sidewalk, counting the squares of cement. She notices that there are about 18 squares in front of each house. If there are 9 houses on each block and she walks 6 blocks, about how many squares of cement does she walk on?

_____

Thursday ⟨35⟩

1. $6.2 - 0.93 = $ _____

2. Write about how to solve this problem.

$$5\frac{1}{2} \div 2\frac{1}{3}$$

_____

_____

_____

3. If the range of this data is 28, what number belongs in the blank?

21, 26, 33, 35, 44, 47, ____

4. What is any number divided by itself (with the exception of zero)?

_____

5. Kyle is trying to figure out how many bricks he needs to build his fort. He wants the fort to be a square with the **inside** dimensions of 4 feet by 4 feet. If each brick is 6 inches long, 3 inches wide, and 2 inches high, what is the least number of bricks needed for the first layer? (There is no door or other break in the wall.)

_____

Friday ⟨35⟩

Jon, Shamika, Jennifer, and Ricardo would like to divide all of their coins so that they each have the same amount of money. They start out with the following:

Jon starts with 2 quarters and 3 pennies.
Shamika starts with 10 dimes and 4 pennies.
Jennifer starts with 4 nickels and 1 quarter.
Ricardo starts with 3 dimes and 16 pennies.

Tell what coins each person will have once the amounts have been made equal.

_____

_____

_____

_____

Daily Math Practice

Daily Progress Record ⟨35⟩

How many did you get correct each day? Color the squares.

	Monday	Tuesday	Wednesday	Thursday	Friday
5					
4					
3					
2					
1					

1. $2\frac{1}{4} \times 1\frac{3}{5} =$ _____

2.
$$\begin{array}{r} (^-6) \\ - \ (^-9) \\ \hline \end{array}$$

3. If $z = 4$, what is the value of $5z + 8$?

_____

4. What is 30% of 450?

_____

5. Raquel has 18 eggs to begin her cooking. She uses half of them in the omelet she makes for breakfast. Then she uses one-third of what is left for some cookies. Then she uses half of what is left for a casserole for supper. How many eggs are left at the end of the day?

_____

1. Correct any mistakes or write "correct."

$2.5 \div 5 = 0.5$ _____

2. Correct any mistakes or write "correct."

$(^-4) + 6 = 10$ _____

3. What is the LCM of 3, 6, and 7?

_____

4. Which of these lettered figures is congruent to the first figure?

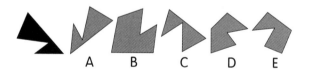

A   B   C   D   E

5. Melanie plays softball and is hitting 30% of the balls pitched to her. If she has hit the softball 39 times, about how many times has the ball been pitched to her?

_____

Wednesday 36

1. Add a sign.

   6 7 8 1 8 9 = 489

2. Add a sign.

   4 9 8 1 2 = 41.5

3. Which is longer: 1 foot, 1 meter, 4 feet, or 38 inches?

   _____

4. How many milliliters are in 2 liters?

   _____

5. Drew trades baseball cards with his friends. He started with 180. He gave 8 to Ted and Ted gave him 12. Then Drew gave Stacy 6 and she gave Drew 5 in return. Finally, Drew gave Alan 18 and Alan gave Drew 24. How many cards did Drew have after all the trading was done? Write the algebraic expression to show the trading.

   _____

Thursday 36

1. $(^-5) - (^-10) =$ _____

2. Write about how to solve this problem.

   $$4\frac{4}{5} \times 3\frac{8}{9}$$

   _____

   _____

3. What is the area of a right triangle whose legs measure 4 cm and 3 cm? Write the equation and solve it.

4. Construct a circle graph for this data. Use a sheet of paper.

Main Course	Percentage
hamburgers	36%
hot dogs	10%
pizza	20%
subs	30%
other	4%

5. Nina is walking her neighbors' dogs while they are on vacation. The Smiths have 2 dogs, the Ortiz family has 3 dogs, and the Valdez family has 1 dog. If Nina can walk only 2 dogs at a time, how many walks does she have to go on to walk each dog once?

   _____

Friday ⟨36⟩

Pick either Figure 1 or Figure 2. How many squares are in that design?

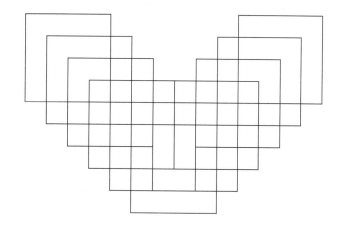 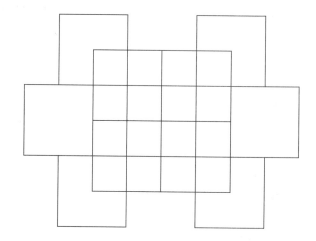

Figure 1   Figure 2

_____   _____

Daily Progress Record ⟨36⟩

How many did you get correct each day? Color the squares.

	Monday	Tuesday	Wednesday	Thursday	Friday
5					
4					
3					
2					
1					

How to Solve
Word Problems

 Read the problem carefully. Think about what it says.

 Look for clue words. The clue words will tell you which operation to use—addition, subtraction, multiplication, or division. Hint: Sometimes you will use more than one operation.

 Solve the problem.

 Check your work. Make sure your answer makes sense.

Clue Words

Add	Subtract	Multiply	Divide
in all	how much more	times	parts
all together	more than	product of	equal parts
total	less than	multiplied by	separated
sum	are left	by (with measurements or dimensions)	divided by
both	take away		quotient of
plus	difference	area	a fraction of
	fewer		average

Monday
1. 54,531
2. 1,515
3. 18 mm (millimeter), 7 cm (centimeter), 3 dm (decimeter), 1 m (meter)
4. A rectangle is a quadrilateral (a figure with four sides) that has four right angles (90° each). Each pair of opposite sides of a rectangle are congruent (exactly the same length) and parallel to each other.
5. $17.93

Tuesday
1. 111
2. 332
3. 1 out of 6 or $\frac{1}{6}$
4. Look for a student's understanding of the base-ten system and how that is implemented in subtraction.
5. $25\frac{1}{2}$ hours

Wednesday
1. 72
2. 28
3. 2:45 P.M.
4. square units
5. 11 toads

Thursday
1. 6
2. 5
3. 32°F
4. Division is the process of breaking apart something into even subgroups.
5. 112 cracks

Friday
The third building would need 10 blocks and would look like the following because a block is added to each side (left and right) and to the top each time.

Monday
1. 2,427
2. 18,131
3. 9
4. Possible answers include:
   1 quarter, 1 dime, and 2 pennies
   1 quarter, 2 nickels, and 2 pennies
   1 quarter, 1 nickel, and 7 pennies
   3 dimes, 1 nickel, and 2 pennies
   3 dimes and 7 pennies
   7 nickels and 2 pennies
   37 pennies
5. $37.62

Tuesday
1. 915
2. 887
3. 6,025
4. 3,700
5. 132 miles

Wednesday
1. 168
2. 9
3.

Input	Output
1	2
2	4
3	6
4	8
5	10
10	20
14	28

4. Answers vary. Because there is one low score, the mean is not in her favor. Mode is good - 182 and median is good - 182.
5. $8.74

Thursday
1. 8
2. 104
3.
4. 144 inches
5. $18

Friday
Sofia will have to make 18 stitches.

Monday
1. 8.99
2. 14.98
3. 15, 18, 21
4. ten-thousands
5. 4 stacks

Tuesday
1. 3.24
2. 5.07
3. 1, 2, 3, 4, 6, 12
4. < (less than)
5. No, because the total needed to ride all three rides would be $1.40 and Raul only has $1.35.

Wednesday
1. 30
2. 24
3. $n = 8$
4. (8, 10)
5. 12 years old

Thursday
1. 6
2. 9
3. Two congruent figures would have the same shape, and the lengths of each side of one shape would correspond to those of the other shape. In other words, if you cut out one of the shapes and laid it directly on top of the other shape, it would match.
4. 15 square inches
5. 5 sticks

Friday
$11.70

Week 4

Monday
1. 158,276
4. 56°
2. 2,431
5. 4 cats
3. 18 cm

Tuesday
1. 4,693
4. 6
2. 3.38
5. 32 goals
3. One possible graph:

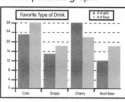

Wednesday
1. 12
5. 7 complete octaves
2. 156
3. 3, 6, 9, 12
4. Possible answers include a baseball, a snowball, a scoop of ice cream, a tomato, and the earth.

Thursday
1. 7
2. 9
3. kilogram
4. It means that the price is reduced by one-fourth, or they save $25 out of every $100 that the jacket originally costs.
5. Amy has 80 CDs and April has 40 CDs.

Friday
425 is the product. Expect many different approaches. For example, a student might write about it in terms of quarters—4 quarters make up a dollar, so 16 quarters make up 4 dollars and one more quarter would make 425. Another student might write about breaking it up—10 seventeens are 170, so 20 seventeens are 340 and then 5 seventeens would be half of 10, or 85. So 25 seventeens would be 340 plus 85.

Week 5

Monday
1. 12.02
2. 15.97
3. 10
4. 4
5. Ryan is 4 and Brandon is 2.

Tuesday
1. 1.11
2. 3.8
3. 27 cubic inches
4. The angle measures 90 degrees and looks like the corner of a book.
5. 6 pizzas

Wednesday
1. 3.6
2. 30
3. 3 out of 6, $\frac{3}{6}$, 1 out of 2, or $\frac{1}{2}$
4. 8
5. 98 minutes or 1 hour and 38 minutes

Thursday
1. 8
2. 24
3. 20 pairs of initials
4. 15
5. 5 feet, 4 inches tall

Friday
She has enough to feed the rabbits for 10 days.

Week 6

Monday
1. 10.12
2. 1,889
3. ○ ○ △
4. 8
5. 18 eyes

Tuesday
1. 6,632
2. 2.21
3. The decimal point divides the whole from the part; the value on the left is the number of whole dollars, while the value on the right is what part of another dollar there is.
4. hundreds
5. 36 minutes

Wednesday
1. 24
2. 800
3. 3 + 5 = 8, 5 + 3 = 8, 8 − 5 = 3, and 8 − 3 = 5
4. B
5. $5.19

Thursday
1. 7
2. 0.60 or 0.6
3. 36,000
4. 3
5. $12.50

Friday
There are many possible answers. Look to see that the axes are labeled and that the student has given some true statements based on the assigned titles. An example could be that these are the temperatures for the first 8 days of January. This student would title the graph "January Temperatures" and label the x-axis with the dates and the y-axis with "Temperatures in Fahrenheit." Some statements might be that the coldest day was on January 4th, while the warmest days were on January 5th and 8th. Students could also make statements about the range of the data or predict what the next day's temperature would be, etc.

Monday
1. 12.39
2. 8.79
3. 10:00 A.M.
4. input multiplied by 4 or f(n) = 4n
5. 28 books

Tuesday
1. 2.43
2. 1.584
3. 13,005
4. 12
5. 30 days

Wednesday
1. 56
2. 4.8
3.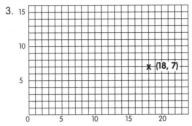
4. 37
5. 33 baseball cards

Thursday
1. 5   4. 15 mm
2. 0.7   5. $1.30
3. 1,000

Friday
900 square inches or $6\frac{1}{4}$ square feet

Monday
1. 17.75
2. 2.053
3.

4. 12
5. $11\frac{1}{2}$ pages or 11.5 pages

Tuesday
1. 721,112
2. 6.31
3. =
4. 1, 2, 4, 8
5. 22 beanbag animals

Wednesday
1. 36
2. 732
3. three hundred seventy-eight
4. tenths
5. 90¢

Thursday
1. 32
2. 24
3. 16, 32, 64
4. D
5. 5:15 P.M.

Friday
4 different ways:
Tim, Sally, Judy, Neal
Neal, Sally, Judy, Tim
Tim, Judy, Sally, Neal
Neal, Judy, Sally, Tim

Monday
1. 14.09
2. 14.505
3. C = 25.12 cm
4. 1 foot, 16 inches, $\frac{1}{2}$ yard, 2 feet, 1 yard
5. 13.5 minutes or $13\frac{1}{2}$ minutes

Tuesday
1. 2.45
2. 5.68
3. 65°F
4. B and C
5. 192 minutes or 3 hours and 12 minutes

Wednesday
1. 45
2. 4,680
3. 6, 12, 18
4. 36,000
5. 2,160 pages

Thursday
1. 6
2. 0.42
3. One possible graph:

4. 8
5. $4\frac{1}{2}$ cups of flour

Friday
Note: A grid has been provided for the first problem of this type. For subsequent problems, if your students are new to logic puzzles, teach them how to set up a labeled grid to track the information given in the clues. Do logic puzzles together initially.
Al—dog, Rocky
Linda—rabbit, Fluffy
Jeff—cat, Chunk

Week 10

Monday
1. ⁻8
2. $\frac{2}{4}$ or $\frac{1}{2}$
3. isosceles triangle
4. 60
5. 300 baseball cards

Tuesday
1. 1.31
2. $\frac{2}{8}$ or $\frac{1}{4}$
3. 1 mg (milligram), 1 g (gram), 1 kg (kilogram)
4. Area = 153.86 in.²
5. 8 inches

Wednesday
1. 3.1
2. ⁻49
3. 26 out of 52, $\frac{26}{52}$, 1 out of 2, or $\frac{1}{2}$
4. 7,000
5. Suzanne is 61 inches tall and Juan is 46 inches tall.

Thursday
1. ⁻8
2. 63
3. 14 square centimeters

4.

5. 6 outfits

Friday
160 mouths and 608 feet (4 men, 4 women, and 8 kids; 24 cats and 120 kittens)

Week 11

Monday
1. $\frac{3}{3}$ or 1
2. $\frac{4}{5}$
3. 24 cubic inches
4. two angles whose sum is 90°
5. $8.75

Tuesday
1. $\frac{2}{9}$
2. $3\frac{2}{7}$
3. hundredths
4. 6 + 3
5. 16 out of 26, $\frac{16}{26}$, 8 out of 13, or $\frac{8}{13}$

Wednesday
1. 0.246
2. 4,200
3. rectangle
4. 21, 25, 29
5. 6: 1, 2, 3, 6
   8: 1, 2, 4, 8
   GCF is 2

Thursday
1. 63
2. > (greater than)
3.
2•2•2•3•5 are the prime factors.

4.

5. yes

Friday
Note: If your students are new to logic puzzles, teach them how to set up a labeled grid to track the information given in the clues. Do logic puzzles together initially.
Cindy Hughes—FL, car
Tim Bartlet—SD, van
Sally Brown—CA, plane
Scott Miller—CO, bus

Week 12

Monday
1. $\frac{7}{8}$
2. ⁻2
3. if the number is even or ends in 0, 2, 4, 6, or 8
4. 2,590,000
5. 48 cans of soup

Tuesday
1. $3\frac{5}{11}$
2. $4\frac{1}{5}$
3. two angles whose sum is 180°
4. Yes, all squares are rectangles. No, all rectangles are not squares.
5. $8

Wednesday
1. 81
2. 0.312
3. 22.5 centimeters
4. 2.93
5. 45 meals

Thursday
1. 9
2. 0.32
3. 28.8 or $28\frac{4}{5}$
4. $m = 3$
5. 192 square inches, $1\frac{1}{3}$ square feet, or 1.3333 square feet

Friday
24 different numbers with the smallest one being 367, because the smallest digit you can have in the hundreds place is the three, followed by the next smallest number in the tens place, and the next smallest number in the ones place.
Note: Students may need to write out all the 3-digit combinations to solve this problem. In discussing the solution, guide students toward discovering shortcuts to solving this type of problem. (There are four possible groups of three digits: 3,6,7; 3,6,9; 3,7,9; 6,7,9. For each of these groups, six 3-digit numbers can be formed. 4 x 6 = 24.)

EMC 755 • © Evan-Moor Corp.

Monday
1. $7\frac{2}{4}$ or $7\frac{1}{2}$
2. 6
3. 89 and 90
4. 12
5. about 2,350 people

Tuesday
1. 6,592
2. $\frac{3}{8}$
3. 12
4.

5. 24

Wednesday
1. $\frac{1}{8}$
2. 20,244
3. 11
4. 16, 15, 19, 18—The pattern is to add 4, subtract 1.
5. 114

Thursday
1. 0.6
2. 418
3. $\frac{1}{2}$ or 1 out of 2
4. $\frac{1}{4}$ or 1 out of 4

5. 16 chickens and 12 horses. 28 heads is a given; each animal has at least 2 legs, so 28 x 2 = 56 legs accounted for. The remaining 24 legs must go to the horses who need 2 more each; 24 ÷ 2 = 12 horses.

Friday

Week 14

Monday
1. 20,650
2. $\frac{3}{4}$
3. 345.6
4. A number is divisible by 5 if it ends in a 5 or a 0.
5. 4 boys and 12 girls

Tuesday
1. 5.282
2. $\frac{1}{4}$
3. 27 blocks
4. 3 and 4
5. 67

Wednesday
1. 609
2. 1.5
3. 62 centimeters
4. input times 3 plus 1 or f(n) = 3n + 1
5. 45 degrees

Thursday
1. 10
2. 0.126
3. Z = 4
4. One possible drawing would be of pies:

5. every 21 days

Friday
There is more than one possible answer. Here is one solution:

$$\begin{array}{r} \boxed{3} \\ \times\ \boxed{2} \\ \hline \boxed{6} \end{array} \qquad \boxed{9} \div 3 = \boxed{3}$$

$$4 + \boxed{1} = \boxed{5} \qquad \begin{array}{r} \boxed{7} \\ \times\ \boxed{4} \\ \hline 2\ \boxed{8} \end{array}$$

Week 15

Monday
1. 17.97
2. $\frac{8}{9}$
3. 9
4. (⁻6, 5) and (⁻3, ⁻4)
5. Alpha Alpha has the better buy because its candy bars are just over 31¢ per candy bar, while the ones from Good Food Warehouse are 33¢ each.

Tuesday
1. 12,274
2. $2\frac{2}{3}$
3. thousandths
4. < (less than)

5. $72 = 2^3 \bullet 3^2$

$$\begin{array}{c} 72 \\ \diagdown \\ 8 \bullet 9 \\ \diagup\diagdown \quad \diagup\diagdown \\ 4 \bullet 2 \quad 3 \bullet 3 \\ \diagup\diagdown \\ 2 \bullet 2 \end{array}$$

Wednesday
1. $\frac{2}{15}$
2. 1.008
3. possible answers: angles *a* and *b*, *a* and *d*, *b* and *c*, *d* and *c*
4. 103.016
5. $18.75 each

Thursday
1. 0.7
2. 82
3. 4 faces
4. 6 out of 6, $\frac{6}{6}$, or 1
5. 512 feet per second

Friday
1, 2, 10, 11, 12, 20, 21, 22, 100, 101

Monday
1. 7
2. $\frac{9}{8}$ or $1\frac{1}{8}$
3. 18.84 cubic inches
4. 2,700.4
5. $82.07

Tuesday
1. 1.947
2. $4\frac{5}{8}$
3. 6
4.

5. Kayleen is wrong. Even though she got tails the first time, her chances of getting heads are still 1 out of 2 or $\frac{1}{2}$ the next time.

Wednesday
1. $\frac{4}{15}$
2. 4,094
3. B
4. 3:00 A.M.
5. 38 minutes

Thursday
1. $\frac{6}{6}$ or 1
2. 4
3. 30, 42, 38

4. rectangle
5. 35 degrees

Friday
Students should label each section of the graph with the name of a TV show and make statements such as:

52.3% of the people preferred "X," which was by far the majority.

The smallest group preferred "Y" with only 9.3%.

Just over a fifth of the class preferred "Z" with 20.9%.

Monday
1. 13.26
2. $8\frac{6}{12}$ or $8\frac{1}{2}$
3. 1,440 minutes in a day
4. 27, 54 (If the sum of the digits is divisible by 3, then the number itself is divisible by 3.)
5. $22\frac{2}{3}$ minutes

Tuesday
1. $5\frac{2}{4}$ or $5\frac{1}{2}$
2. $\frac{3}{12}$ or $\frac{1}{4}$
3. all of them
4. 540 inches
5. $598.50

Wednesday
1. $\frac{2}{21}$
2. $\frac{77}{8}$ or $9\frac{5}{8}$
3. 3 + (2 + 4)
4. 32 ounces in 1 quart
5. 155 minutes or 2 hours and 35 minutes

Thursday
1. $\frac{28}{10}$, $2\frac{8}{10}$, or $2\frac{4}{5}$
2. 0.252
3. triangle
4. 30
5. 137.5 miles

Friday
5, 8, 11, 14, 17, **20**, **23** (add 3 each time)
1, 1, 2, 3, 5, 8, **13**, **21** (Fibonacci numbers—add the previous two numbers)
2, 6, 18, 54, **162**, **486** (multiply by 3 each time)
M, T, W, T, F, **S**, **S** (first letter of the days of the week)
F, S, T, F, F, S, **S**, **E** (first letter of the ordinals)
A, M, J, J, A, S, **O**, **N** (first letter of the months starting with April)

Monday
1. 9
2. $\frac{7}{12}$
3. 0
4. 296,000,000
5. One possible graph:

Tuesday
1. 9,971
2. $5\frac{11}{12}$
3. The estimate should be at least in the ten-thousands place—If you round 903 to 900 and 29 to 30, then a better estimate would be 27,000.

4. 95 degrees
5. 188 minutes or 3 hours and 8 minutes

Wednesday
1. 0.0468
2. $\frac{144}{35}$ or $4\frac{4}{35}$
3. 136 square mm
4. 120 (Allow students to act this out or use manipulatives.)
5. 13, 15, and 17

Thursday
1. $\frac{15}{16}$
2. 2.635
3. 86
4. 24
5. $1\frac{3}{4}$ hours, 1 hour and 45 minutes, or 105 minutes

Friday
Possible answers include:

Dimensions	Area
11 cm x 1 cm	11 cm²
10 cm x 2 cm	20 cm²
9 cm x 3 cm	27 cm²
8 cm x 4 cm	32 cm²
7 cm x 5 cm	35 cm²
6 cm x 6 cm	36 cm²

Answers may also include fractions and/or decimals such as:

10.5 cm x 1.5 cm	15.75 cm²

Monday
1. 640
2. 8,651
3. rhombus (parallelogram, quadrilateral)
4. $\frac{97}{4}$
5. 22 oz. for $1.10

Tuesday
1. 8 x 12 = 96
2. 0.7 x 8 = 5.6
3. 1, 2, 3, 5, 6, 10, 15, 30
4. 2, 3, 5, 7, and 11
5. 110 feet

Wednesday
1. 136 + 59
2. 52 x 10
3. 96 ounces
4. 0.08
5. B and F

Thursday
1. $\frac{8}{15}$
2. One possible answer: To subtract decimals, you need to line up the decimals. Then you will need to borrow from the whole number to have enough tenths to subtract 9.
3. 9 degrees
4. 6 & 1, 5 & 2, and 4 & 3

5. Fill the 3-quart pitcher and pour it into the 5-quart pitcher. Fill the 3-quart pitcher again and pour it into the 5-quart pitcher until the 5-quart pitcher is full. What remains in the 3-quart pitcher is 1 quart.

Friday
Jimmy's number could be 54, 66, 72, 78, 84, or 96. Answers for the remaining part will vary.

Monday
1. 11.2
2. 116,196
3. three hundred fifty-two and eight tenths
4. $23\frac{1}{2}$ or 23.5
5. 15 handshakes (Assign 6 students the first 6 letters of the alphabet and act this out.)

Tuesday
1. correct
2. 5.3 − 0.7 = 4.6
3. no
4. yes
5. Friday he earned $10, Saturday he earned $20, and Sunday he earned $40.

Wednesday
1. 1,962 ÷ 18 = 109
2. 962 − 529 = 433
3. tens
4. 72
5. 4 socks

Thursday
1. 39.90
2. One possible answer: Ask how many times 5 goes into 8. The rest (3) could be called a remainder or you can add the decimal and zeros and divide until you get it to come out even.
3. 37

4. $n = 4$
5. 160 seconds or 2 minutes, 40 seconds

Friday
2,764,800 blades of grass in the lawn

Monday
1. 3,240
2. $5\frac{7}{9}$
3. 44
4. 216 cubic centimeters
5. 16 units

Tuesday
1. 256 − 57 = 199
2. $\frac{1}{2} + \frac{1}{4} = \frac{3}{4}$
3. 40
4. > (greater than)
5. Marissa's claim is partly accurate. Yes, the average length of her phone calls was about 6 minutes, but the number of phone calls was only six instead of fifteen. Therefore she was only on the phone 36 minutes each night instead of the 90 minutes that she claimed.

Wednesday
1. 24 x 12 = 288
2. 9,625 − 807 = 8,818
3. 6
4. D
5. 1,345 feet

Thursday
1. $\frac{3}{10}$

2. One possible answer: Compute each of these subproducts: 4 x 6 = 24, 4 x 20 = 80, 10 x 6 = 60, 10 x 20 = 200; then add up the subproducts.
3. 135 minutes
4. 12%
5. about $6.67

Friday
once every 70 days

Monday
1. 1
2. 0.3 or 0.30
3. It is a negative sign, which means that the temperature is below zero.
4. input times 5
5. just under 8 minutes

Tuesday
1. correct
2. 0.3 x 0.2 = 0.06
3.
4. 6
5. about 167 seconds or 2 minutes and 47 seconds

Wednesday
1. 665 ÷ 25 = 26.6
2. 978 + 842 = 1,820
3. 2 x 5
4. 2,000
5. Joseph will clean 8 rooms and Chandra will clean 4 rooms.

Thursday
1. 6.4
2. ⁻9
3. See student work for three acute angles such as the following:

4. (⁻8, 2) and (6, ⁻4)
5. 80 feet

Friday
Some students may use trial and error; others may find that the numbers add up to 45, divide this by 3, and determine that the sum in every direction must be 15. One possibility is:

8	1	6
3	5	7
4	9	2

Monday
1. 3.16
2. $3\frac{1}{12}$
3. eight hundred twenty-six
4. 20,000
5. Pierre has 1 quarter, 3 dimes, 5 nickels, and 2 pennies.

Tuesday
1. correct
2. correct
3. 1, 5, 25—5 should be circled
4. none
5. 1,080

Wednesday
1. 632 ÷ 8 = 79
2. 456 x 9 = 4,104
3. ⁻6°F
4. Answers may include A, C, E, T, and W, among others.
5. 36 blocks—It has the same view from each of the four corners.

Thursday
1. $\frac{3}{4}$
2. One possible answer: Since the 9 doesn't have a decimal marked, it is assumed to be to the right of it, meaning it is a whole number. Next, line up the decimals and write the numbers vertically over each other. Then you will need to borrow 10 tenths from the 9 so you can subtract the 6 tenths. Finally, subtract and bring the decimal point straight down.

3. mean–88, median–88, mode–88
4. 31
5. Each gets 7 balloons. Then the students can be creative with what happens with the last three balloons, but they should realize that they can't cut them up and each get three-fifths of a balloon.

Friday

Region	Number	Color
A	4	brown
B	5	green
C	2	blue
D	3	orange
E	1	red
F	6	purple

Monday
1. $\frac{9}{20}$
2. 4.94
3. Accept a range of answers from 14 to 17, as long as students can explain how they got their estimates.
4. 8
5. 20 years old

Tuesday
1. correct
2. $1\frac{1}{3}$ x 3 = 4
3. ten-thousandths
4. 15
5. about 1,350 words

Wednesday
1. 552 + 658 = 1,210
2. 996 – 35 = 961
3. 8
4. 88.3
5. No, he does not have enough money yet. He has $350, but he needs $370.

Thursday
1. $1\frac{13}{35}$
2. One possible answer: Ask how many times 3 goes into 10. The rest (1) could be called a remainder or you could represent it as a fraction ($\frac{1}{3}$).

3. 21,120 feet
4. 24
5. $19.58

Friday
A reasonable prediction might be 270 to 290. Most weeks seem to be increasing by about 30, but this growth is beginning to level off, so the gain may not be as high at week 6. (**Note:** You might plot the data on a line graph to see the trend.)

EMC 755 • © Evan-Moor Corp.

Monday
1. ⁻324
2. $\frac{29}{21}$ or $1\frac{8}{21}$
3. $s = 21$
4. 0
5. 24 kids

Tuesday
1. correct
2. 126 – 99 = 27
3. 7,026
4. 97,000
5. 20 seconds

Wednesday
1. 26 × 912 = 23,712
2. 4,632 ÷ 8 = 579
3. 1 and 2
4. 32 quarts
5. 6 ways

Thursday
1. 4.6
2. One possible answer: Compute each of these subproducts: 2 × 9 = 18, 2 × 40 = 80, 10 × 9 = 90, 10 × 40 = 400; then add up the subproducts.
3. 20 feet
4. 33
5. 370 miles west of where it started out

Friday

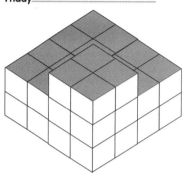

Monday
1. 10
2. 88
3. 33
4.
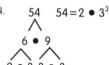
$54 = 2 \bullet 3^3$
5. $\frac{5}{26}$ or $\frac{6}{26} = \frac{3}{13}$ (depending on whether y is included as a vowel) 10 or 12 (depending on whether y is included as a vowel)

Tuesday
1. $2\frac{1}{3} - \frac{2}{3} = 1\frac{2}{3}$
2. 49 ÷ 0.7 = 70
3. 364 and 1,093
4. $x = 15$
5. 32 fence posts

Wednesday
1. 987 – 111 = 876
2. 126 ÷ 5 = 25.2
3. angles B and C
4. 36 cubic centimeters
5. 8 ounces

Thursday
1. 34
2. One possible answer: Multiply 5 times 2. Then count how many digits are to the right of the decimal place in both numbers. Since there are two digits to the right of the decimals, you need 2 digits to the right of the decimal in the answer.
3. 168
4. associative property of addition
5. 38 people

Friday
72 square feet, 3 cans of spray paint

Monday
1. 5
2. $3\frac{3}{8}$
3. Many possible answers, including 2.4, 2.84, $2\frac{1}{2}$, $2\frac{7}{100}$, etc.
4. 4, 6, 8, 9, 10
5. 2 inches

Tuesday
1. correct
2. 25 – 1.3 = 23.7
3. ⁻4

4.

Input	Output
1	9
2	12
5	21
8	30
12	42

5. $\frac{4}{3}$ or $1\frac{1}{3}$ quarts

Wednesday
1. 12 + 964 = 976
2. 865 ÷ 5 = 173
3. 10,000
4. Possible answers include 0, 3, 8, 33.
5. $26.25

Thursday
1. $\frac{3}{6}$ or $\frac{1}{2}$
2. One possible answer: Ask how many times 7 goes into 12. The rest (5) could be called a remainder or you could represent it as a fraction ($\frac{5}{7}$).
3. obtuse angles
4. 17 pounds, 2 ounces
5. about 210 cans

Friday
Many possible answers, including circle, triangle, acute angle, point, line segment, radius, etc.

Monday
1. $1\frac{3}{4}$
2. 25.03
3. 1
4.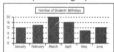
5. The second route through Canon City and Grover is shorter by 17 miles.

Tuesday
1. correct
2. correct
3. about 7 miles
4. 6
5. 13.1%

Wednesday
1. 325 + 862 = 1,187
2. 49 + 6,598 = 6,647
3. cylinder   20 sq. in.
4. 81 degrees
5. 3 ounces

Thursday
1. 696.49
2. One possible answer: Change the mixed numbers into improper fractions. Then multiply numerators and write that on the top of the fraction. Multiply denominators and write that on the bottom of the fraction. Next, reduce or simplify if necessary.

3. 7
4. any two numbers that add up to 17 (e.g., 10 & 7 or 12 & 5)
5. 63 bats

Friday
(5, 12)

Monday
1. 1.05
2. 1,015,144
3. 3
4. One possible graph:

Number of Students' Birthdays

5. 208 mice

Tuesday
1. 56 ÷ 8 = 7
2. 2.4 + 0.13 = 2.53
3. 400,000
4. Possible answers: angles *a* and *b*, *b* and *c*, *c* and *d*, *d* and *a*
5. 210 pounds

Wednesday
1. 7,335 ÷ 15 = 489
2. 26 x 82 = 2,132
3. decagon
4. 42 cm
5. Jim is 12 years old, his father is 43 years old, and his grandfather is 82 years old. (Expect students to arrive at these answers by trial and error.)

Thursday
1. 5.55
2. One possible answer: First change the mixed numbers into improper fractions. Then change the division to multiplication and flip the second fraction (write its reciprocal). Next, multiply numerators and write that on the top of the

fraction. Multiply denominators and write that on the bottom of the fraction. Then reduce or simplify if necessary.
3. 15
4. 1.2 square inches
5. 30 triangles

Friday
The sale price of the model car is $5 and the sale price of the model truck is $8. The original price of the model car is $10 and the original price of the model truck is $16.

Monday
1. $\frac{18}{25}$
2. 4.96
3. 3:00 P.M.
4. 30 degrees
5. Yes, they both could be correct. For example, if the answer was 452, Carlos could round to the nearest hundred, while Julie could round to the nearest ten.

Tuesday
1. $\frac{1}{3} \div \frac{1}{2} = \frac{2}{3}$
2. 0.5 x 0.1 = 0.05
3. 16
4. 2 out of 6, $\frac{2}{6}$, 1 out of 3, or $\frac{1}{3}$ 20 times

5. Possible answers include:
   1.2 x 2 = 2.4
   2.5 − 0.1 = 2.4
   9.6 ÷ 4 = 2.4
   1.3 + 1.1 = 2.4

Wednesday
1. 496 − 189 = 307
2. 2 x 496 = 992
3. *m* = 0
4. 36
5. 40 blocks

Thursday
1. ⁻6
2. One possible answer: Compute each of the subproducts: 9 x 7 = 63, 9 x 20 = 180, 50 x 7 = 350, 50 x 20 = 1,000. Then add up the subproducts.
3. 16
4. 51 feet
5. $10.61

Friday
Liz ran farther because she ran 21,120 feet, while Josh only ran 18,000 feet.

Monday
1. 0.315
2. 15,366
3. 27 cm
4. $\frac{4}{98}$
5. 19.5 inches or $19\frac{1}{2}$ inches

Tuesday
1. correct
2. 1,964 + 2,043 = 4,007
3. 8 cups
4. two hundred fifty-eight
5. your friend with spinner B

Wednesday
1. 1,130 ÷ 25 = 45.2
2. 9,000 ÷ 100 = 90
3. 72 cubic inches
4. itself (1 · x = x)
5. about 1,440 band members

Thursday
1. $7\frac{5}{6}$
2. One possible answer: If you think of this problem in terms of temperature, you would be taking away cold; then the temperature is going to go up 4 degrees, so you add 3 and 4.
3. > (greater than)

4. D
5. Herman is 7 years old.

Friday
She needs 271 toothpicks to build 90 squares. She can build 333 squares with 1,000 toothpicks. The pattern is taking the number of squares and multiplying it by 3 and adding 1 more. If you are given the number of toothpicks, subtract 1 and then divide by 3.

Monday
1. 140.2
2. ⁻13
3. 25
4. HELLO | O⅃⅃ƎH
5. L + G = 15, L • G = 56
   Leda is 8 years old and Ginger is 7 years old.

Tuesday
1. 6 × 8 = 48
2. correct
3. There are many possible answers; must have 8 numbers listed and have the number 6 appearing most frequently.
4. While 12 square units is the exact answer, accept a range of 11 to 13.
5. 11:00 P.M.

Wednesday
1. 4,692 + 52 = 4,744
2. 462 × 18 = 8,316
3. 24
4. 19 feet
5. 2 quarters, 3 nickels, and 3 pennies

Thursday
1. ⁻11
2. One possible answer: If you think about debt and you are taking away 2 dollars of debt, your debt will lessen by 2, so subtract the 2 from 8, but you need to keep the negative sign in the answer because you are still in debt.
3. 390,000

4. 1, 2, 3, 6, 9, 18—2 and 3 should be circled
5. Emily has 16 dolls and Holly has 23 dolls. E + H = 39, E = H − 7, or E + 7 = H

Friday
Here is one possible answer: If you round 49 to 50 and think of 19 fifties, it would add up to 950. Then you need to subtract 19 because we want 49 of them instead of 50. That gives you 931.

Monday
1. ⁻7
2. 4
3. 4° Fahrenheit
4. 1 pound
5. 6 paths

Tuesday
1. correct
2. $2\frac{1}{5} + 3\frac{2}{3} = 5\frac{13}{15}$
3. a circle
4. 180 degrees
5. 3

Wednesday
1. 456 − 92 = 364
2. 91 ÷ 455 = 0.2

3.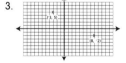
4. input minus 4
5. level 31

Thursday
1. 1,107,128
2. One possible answer: Rewrite the fractions as like fractions, using 14 as the denominator. If you can't subtract $\frac{7}{14}$, you need to borrow $\frac{14}{14}$ from the 5. Then subtract the whole numbers, subtract the numerators, and write the difference over 14.
3. 6
4. 6, 12, 18

5. The following are all possibilities:
   1 touchdown, 1 2-point conversion, and 1 safety
   1 touchdown, 1 point after touchdown, and a field goal
   1 touchdown and 2 safeties
   2 field goals and 2 safeties
   5 safeties

Friday
Many answers are possible. One might be to title the graph "Average Test Scores Out of 50 Points." One line could be labeled for boys and the other for girls, with the x-axis being labeled Week 1, 2, 3, etc. Statements might be: "The boys outperformed the girls on 2 of the weeks," or "On the last week, the boys and girls had the same average."

Monday
1. 6
2. $7\frac{19}{20}$
3. 11 (19–8)
4. 2,500; 12,500; 62,500 (input times 5)
5. 2

Tuesday
1. correct
2. 80
3. pentagon
4. $x = 4$
5. 18 combinations (Encourage students to head a column for each activity and then make an organized list.)

Wednesday
1. 762 – 10 = 752
2. 900 ÷ 30 = 30
3. angles a and c or b and d
4. 30 cubic meters
5. 6 emus and 12 alpacas; solve in same manner as Week 13, Thursday, #5

Thursday
1. 2
2. One possible answer: Multiply 35 times 9. Count the digits to the right of the decimal place in the numbers (3). The answer needs 3 digits to the right of the decimal.

3. 3 pencils for 40¢
4. 653.5
5. 89

Friday

Region	Number	Color
A	3	green
B	5	purple
C	9	brown
D	8	orange
E	1	yellow
F	6	blue
G	4	pink

Monday
1. $\frac{18}{49}$
2. 0.3915
3. input times 2 minus 1 or $f(n) = 2n - 1$
4. 122, 123, 124
5. 12 stamps

Tuesday
1. correct
2. $8 - (\text{˜}2) = 10$
3. 358,000,000
4. 4
5. $38.92

Wednesday
1. 47 x 103 = 4,841
2. 17,962 + 93 = 18,055
3. sphere

4. 54 feet
5. 972 squares

Thursday
1. 5.27
2. One possible answer: First change the mixed numbers into improper fractions. Then change the division to multiplication and flip the second fraction (write its reciprocal). Next, multiply numerators and write that on the top of the fraction. Multiply denominators and write that on the bottom of the fraction. Then reduce or simplify if necessary.
3. 49
4. 1

5. 34 bricks (Answers of 32 may be common; diagram will clarify.)

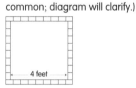
4 feet

Friday
One possibility is:
Person 1 gets 6 dimes and 2 pennies.
Person 2 gets 2 quarters, 1 nickel, and 7 pennies.
Person 3 gets 4 dimes, 2 nickels, and 12 pennies.
Person 4 gets 1 quarter, 3 dimes, 1 nickel, and 2 pennies.

Monday
1. $\frac{72}{20}$, $\frac{18}{5}$, or $3\frac{3}{5}$
2. 3
3. 28
4. 135
5. 3 eggs

Tuesday
1. correct
2. (˜4) + 6 = 2
3. 42
4. A
5. Allow estimated answers; 130 is the exact answer.

Wednesday
1. 678 – 189 = 489
2. 498 ÷ 12 = 41.5
3. 4 feet
4. 2,000
5. 189 cards   180 – 8 + 12 – 6 + 5 – 18 + 24

Thursday
1. 5
2. One possible answer: First change the mixed numbers into improper fractions. Then multiply numerators and write that result on the top of the fraction. Multiply denominators and write that result on the bottom of the fraction. Then reduce or simplify if necessary.

3. 6 square centimeters $A = \frac{1}{2}bh$ $A = \frac{1}{2} \cdot 4 \cdot 3$ $A = 2 \cdot 3 = 6$
4. One possible graph:

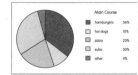

5. 3 walks

Friday
Figure 1 has 101 squares (44 1 x 1 squares, 26 2 x 2 squares, 14 3 x 3 squares, 15 4 x 4 squares, and 2 5 x 5 squares). Figure 2 has 36 squares.